MW01502660

Race Training

with Jim Saltonstall

Race
Training

with Jim Saltonstall

ADLARD COLES NAUTICAL

London

Acknowledgements

I would like to offer my sincere thanks to the following people for all their help in producing this book: First, my wife Christine for all her hard work in putting the manuscript together and converting it into proper English; Dr David Gorrod, RYA medical officer, for his input and support with the chapter on self preparation; Peter Falconer (Pixel Pete!) for all the photography in the book and the many hours he spent braving the elements to get the shots; and Ben Ainslie for kindly writing the Foreword. Finally, I would like to thank Seldén and Super Spars for allowing me to use their mast selection guides.

Published by Adlard Coles Nautical
an imprint of A & C Black Publishers Ltd
38 Soho Square, London W1D 3HB
www.adlardcoles.com

Copyright © Jim Saltonstall 1983, 1990, 1996, 2006
Ben Ainslie photographs copyright © 2004 Rick Tomlinson

First edition published as *RYA Race Training Manual*
by William Heinemann Ltd, 1983
Second edition published by Macmillan Press Ltd 1990
Third edition published as *The RYA Book of Race Training*
by Adlard Coles Nautical 1996
This edition published 2006

ISBN-10: 0-7136-7479-2
ISBN-13: 978-0-7136-7479-8

A CIP catalogue record for this book is available from the British Library.

A & C Black uses paper produced with elemental chlorine-free pulp, harvested from managed sustainable forests.

Book design by Susan McIntyre
Index by Indexing Specialists (UK) Ltd
Typeset in 11 on 13pt Rotis Sans Serif
Printed and bound in China

Note: While all reasonable care has been taken in the publication of this book, the publisher takes no responsibility for the use of the methods or products described in the book.

Contents

Foreword

If there is any one person responsible for the success of the current generation of British sailors, it is Jim Saltonstall. Jim's 30 years' experience, coaching at the top level, gives the reader an invaluable insight in training techniques and coaching methods to prepare for a regatta.

Race training gives you the opportunity to smooth out the weak areas and properly prepare for the upcoming event. If the training is well structured and fun then improvements will come quickly.

Whatever the level, *Race Training with Jim Saltonstall* is a must-have for any racing sailor!

Good sailing.

Ben Ainslie

Ben Ainslie won the 2004 Olympic gold in the Finn class, picked up gold and silver in the Laser class at the 2000 and 1996 Olympics respectively, and has been World and European champion numerous times over the last decade.

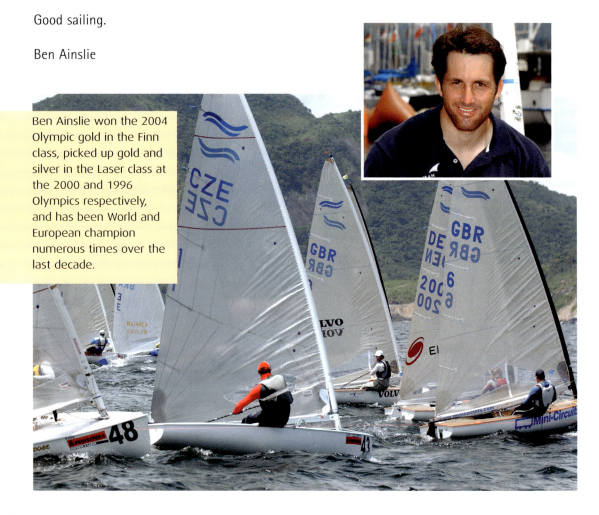

Introduction

The most challenging sport in the world requires a degree of commitment to achieve your ultimate aim, whether that is to win your club championship, the America's Cup or anything in between. When you have decided what it is you wish to achieve, you then have to decide when you want to achieve it and how you are going to achieve it. Establishing what it is you would like to win will help you decide how much commitment will be required in terms of your time – ie arranging your racing/training time around your domestic and social life and also how much of a financial commitment you are willing to make. Deciding on which level of the sport you wish to succeed in will then determine the number of days needed to be put aside for training around education or work and also holidays!

Time management can be a real issue, balancing the number of training days versus event days versus education/working/social days. So a certain amount of time management planning is always required late in the year in readiness for the following year's events. The number of days required for training varies depending on what level of competition you wish to do well in. The number of days' training required to be the club champion will not be as many as those required to win the America's Cup or at least it should not be! Of course, this depends on the standard of racing at your club which, if very high, will require a higher level of commitment to the number of training days required to win the event.

Be realistic. Are you capable of achieving what you are setting out to do? Set realistic targets and adopt the mindset that you are capable of winning if everything goes your way! Whatever level your racing is at, I hope that the contents of this edition of *Race Training* will assist you in achieving your ultimate aim in the most challenging sport in the world.

Never forget that sailing is **fun**; enjoy it first and consider your performance second. Pace yourself. Never put yourself into the position where you get burned out. If you do, take time out and come back to sailing later carrying on from where you left off – refreshed.

To win at any level of competition you will need to be operating to at least 80 per cent efficiency in all 10 aspects of the sport, at times even higher in some aspects. Our sport, like all the others, is about trying not to make mistakes. Of course, everyone makes mistakes, even winners, but they make fewer than the guy who is second and so on down the results sheet! Identify your mistakes and eliminate them from your programme. While in the training mode, identify your strengths and weaknesses, and try to turn your weaknesses into strengths while maintaining your strengths.

Focus on both boat balance and trim. The helmsman should be to windward to assist the boat balance, and this will also help to keep the spinnaker clear of the mainsail. Do not sail too deep an angle in light winds – not good for boat speed!

1
Categories of Preparation

Why do I consider sailing to be the most challenging sport, even more challenging than climbing Mount Everest? Because to achieve the ultimate objective in our sport there are far more categories of preparation (ie variables) than in any other. These variables are:

- **Self preparation**.
- **Boat preparation**.
- **Boat handling**.
- **Boat tuning**.
- **Race strategy**.
- **Starting**.
- **Tactics**.
- **Racing rules**.
- **Compass work**.
- **Meteorology**.

How do you overcome all of these variables? You need:

- **Mileage**.
- **Knowledge**.
- **Experience**.

As with most sports, the age of National, European, World and Olympic Champions is being lowered by the introduction of Youth Training Programmes. For years, youngsters between the ages of five and eight have been introduced to sail training. Continuing on from then, race training has produced Olympic Medallists at the age of nineteen.

Anyone wishing to be a champion in sport must develop a training programme not only around their educational or working careers but also their domestic lives. Normally this would be developed in conjunction with family and a coach, either the class or personal coach.

Youngsters tend to believe that sport comes first, and that education comes second. Wrong! It is the other way round, and we must never forget that. Some also believe that in order to be a champion, you must be a full-time sailor. Wrong again. In fact, in many cases, the full-time sailor is often not the winner of the major events in the world today. You must have other things going on in your life which will take your mind away from competing from time to time, otherwise you just become brain dead and burned out.

Developing a programme

Short, medium, or long-term programmes need to be developed methodically in good time. You should include both your training and events calendar, backdated from the event that you would like to win, or do well in. The minimum time required to prepare for an event is four months in the dinghy world. This could easily be extended to 12 months plus in the yachting world. Your training programme will include all the variables and having completed this you will be in a position where, mentally, you are able to go to the event and do well. Never put yourself in the position where you **expect** to do well, or win. If you do, you are in danger of becoming overconfident and that is the time when mistakes are made or things go wrong.

In addition to developing your training programme in readiness for an event, you have also to look at all the other campaign issues, such as:

- Finance.
- Travel.
- Accommodation.
- Insurance.

This is where a valuable friend or spouse comes into the framework, as all these issues should not be left to competitors. The less involved athletes are in the organisation of travel etc, the better, so they can keep focused on their training programme and preparing in a professional manner ready for the big event.

Never forget the five 'P's:
Perfect
Preparation
Produces
Perfect
Performance

2
Self Preparation

How fit do you need to be? Answer – fit enough to sail as hard on the last leg of the course of the last race, as you did on the first leg of the course of the first race in the upper wind range – and survive the social programme!

Does this mean that you have to be a super-fit human being? No – but you must be as fit as the opposition or have the psychological knowledge that you are among the fittest in the fleet. I have seen someone, who I believed to be the fittest in the fleet, lose a championship because he was going very fast in the wrong direction! Championship racing these days tends to comprise two or three races a day (sometimes more!). Therefore emphasis must be placed on mobility and flexibility as well as stamina because of the smaller courses with shorter legs, more mark roundings and more races in total – maybe 12 races in a championship!

How long does it take to become fit enough to win an event? Answer – it takes a minimum of three months to get fit and only a blink of an eye to become unfit. That is why coaches like to wrap their athletes in cotton wool between events, and only get them out when it is time to perform! It is during this time frame that all other 'inferior sports' are out of the equation as many injuries (around 50 per cent) occur away from sailing. For example, cycling, football, snowboarding, skiing – even dancing – should all be avoided pre-event.

Personal health and prevention of illness are uppermost. There is nothing worse for an athlete or his coach when, after months of training, the competitor picks up either a sports injury or a medical virus sometime during a campaign which reduces their ability to perform. To prevent picking up an infection, try to avoid contact with other 'sick' people and be very 'fussy' about cleanliness especially your feet, eyes and ears and make sure that you frequently wash all your sailing gear. Falling ill or picking up an injury is a complete waste of all the training, money and effort that has been put into the pre-championship preparation.

Before even thinking about winning a major sailing event, look very hard at the following issues remembering the type of boat in which you wish to do well:

- ❏ **Body weight**.
- ❏ **Strength**.
- ❏ **Stamina**.
- ❏ **Flexibility**.
- ❏ **Mobility**.
- ❏ **Agility**.

The most critical of all these perhaps is body weight. How many times do we see the wrong body in the wrong boat, so they cannot possibly be competitive, across the wind range, especially in the light to medium displacement boats. Fitness training plays a major role in yacht and dinghy racing today and is top of the pile in our list of preparation categories: **only the fittest, both physically and mentally, will win.**

At the end of the day you must be able to move around the ship like a mouse wearing carpet slippers and not like a herd of elephants! The type of fitness programme will depend on your job on the ship and even what type of ship you will be sailing. For example, the fitness training programme of a Finn sailor will not resemble anything like that of a 420 crew or that of the helmsman of an IMX 40! Bearing this in mind, it could be well worth your while 'putting your hand in your pocket' and visiting a good physiotherapist to ensure that any fitness training programme you embark on will be the right one for you. In the final week of training, you should be winding down physical work, just doing enough to keep you on your toes and flexible, as you are now building up to the event and need to conserve your energy in readiness for the first race.

Always remember: *Never go into your training programme cold – warm up and stretch out first*. On completion of the session, *warm down – ease out of it; do not just stop and sit or lie down*. If your muscles tend to be tight, re-warm and re-stretch them at the end of your training session.

Stretching and warm-up

Over the years, the value of stretching as sports injury prevention and aid to increased performance has become increasingly recognised.

In the past, stretching was ballistic, meaning that limbs were in motion in ever-increasing arcs; the aim was to try to reach further each time. Eventually it was recognised that this could be a recipe for injury, since limbs are heavy and hard to stop without a jerk. Now, slow careful stretch exercises are recommended. You should never start an exercise programme without a thorough warm-up. In a

With so many variables, you must allow for time in the classroom to learn the theory of the most challenging sport in the world before you put it into practice!

tracksuit this may take time, but in sailing gear, which is designed for heat retention, it does not take so long. Once warm, you can adopt one of the several positions illustrated (pages 16–17), holding the posture so that the muscle to be stretched feels uncomfortably tight but *not* painful in any way. Hold this position for a total of 30 seconds broken into three bouts of 10-second holds with a 2-second gap between each. During the 2-second breaks you should relax to rest the muscles.

You may notice that during the second 10 seconds, you can stretch further than during the first bout. The third stretch may also achieve further stretch. However, during the total 30 seconds, do not push yourself too far and go from uncomfortably stretched to painful, to very painful. The sensation should be from uncomfortably stretched, to uncomfortably stretched, to uncomfortably stretched. Stretch your hamstrings as well as the quads. You will use them – low back pain is frequently associated with tight hamstrings which affect the tilt of the pelvis to which the lower back is attached.

Prior to sailing

To warm up the body, to encourage the heart to a greater output in order to supply and warm the muscles that are going to do the work, it is essential to have a preliminary warm-up routine. This should take place before going on the water and be repeated on the water. A stretch routine during warm-up is mandatory. It used to be said that the effort of launching a Finn over a shingle beach causes greater heart

Fitness Test

Name	Sit-ups max 2 mins	Squat thrusts max 1 min	Burpees max 1 min	Press-ups max	Distance run/swum 12 mins
Sarah	103	96	37	70	21 laps run
Sally	112	89	24	62	18 lengths swum
Ben	108	136	37	50	27 lengths swum
Iain	100	158	47	55	23.5 laps run
Paul	73	93	33	34	21.75 laps run
Penny	95	122	36	56	37.75 lengths swum
Richard	105	80	34	55	27 lengths swum

rate than sailing it! After changing into sailing clothing (which should be adjusted to give full and free movement in every plane) the warm-up should commence. A warm-up routine is required even in warm weather. Professional athletes in track and field would not dream of competing without a prolonged warm-up even on a hot day. It follows that the core temperature of the body will rise unduly if protective clothing is very efficient and each day therefore the duration of warm-up, and the composition of your clothing, will require thought.

After warm-up the muscles are now prepared and ready for stretching exercises. These should be done before launching the dinghy, and they are designed to put the joints through a full range of movement so that the limbs are prepared for any undue stress at the extreme range of motion, without trauma to the joint or over-stretched muscle.

Strengthening exercises consist of several types of muscle toning or building exercises. The individual sailor has to decide whether an overall increase in muscle bulk is required or, if there is already a problem with body weight, whether some fat can usefully be exchanged for muscle.

Fitness training

All serious competitors appreciate that to achieve good results some kind of fitness training is essential. How much training you do obviously depends on your time available and motivation but it can tie in with other favoured sports. Three sessions a week of cycling, jogging or swimming (20-30 minutes' hard work) will improve your overall stamina and endurance. Some sailors do each of these activities once a week if they do not have a problem with their body weight. Keep a regular check on your weight as your programme progresses as, for some sailors (dinghy and small keel boats), this will be a fairly critical factor. *Do not train if you are feeling unwell or have a sore throat or high temperature.*

Midway through your programme, take a fitness test and another one towards the end to compare your improvement and target figures in relation to past squads and teams. Some fitness test results of past squads and teams are shown opposite.

Exhausting fitness training must stop seven days before Race 1 of the championship but continue with a light daily fitness routine in readiness for the event.

Training to win

Physical fitness increases mental fitness; mental fitness increases confidence, and confidence means confidence to **win**. You do not need to be super-fit to be a world champion; being the fittest person on the water does not mean that you are going to win races (do not forget that there are nine other aspects to the sport). I was given the following quotation which I think sums it up perfectly: 'If you don't have the necessary racing skills, physical fitness alone won't make you win races – it just means you will be able to sail badly more comfortably for longer.'

I have known some yachting athletes to be so fit that they cannot sit still in the boat in light weather races because their muscles start twitching, and each time they move they disturb the rig. 'As a rule the best training is achieved simply by carrying out the activity for which one is training' (P O Astrand). In other words, runners must run, swimmers must swim, and dinghy sailors must sail dinghies etc. Can the dinghy sailor who wants to compete at the top level get both the amount and intensity of physical training necessary for success at that level just by sailing? In theory the answer is 'yes', but not if economy of time, effort and expense are important factors in his budget. Before trying to justify that answer we need to appreciate that 'fitness' is not an absolute term, it can only be described relative to a specified activity. We also need to have at least a basic understanding of two principles of training: those of 'overload' and 'specificity'.

Why is fitness relative? Suppose we are asked: 'Are you fit enough to jog a mile?' Most of us would probably answer 'yes'. However, if we were asked: 'Are you fit enough to compete in a 100 metre race against Justin Gatlin or Maurice Greene?' few of us would hesitate to answer 'no'. Here our fitness is being assessed relative to the activity of running and relative to the standards of top-class runners in two different events. Our interest is in fitness, not relative to running but to the demands of racing a single- or double-handed dinghy.

Overload

What do we mean by 'overload'? Our bodies adapt, over time, to the type and intensity of load to which we subject them. If you take on a new activity, or the same activity at an increased intensity, then at first your body will be overloaded. It will not be able to cope without suffering some pain. However, if you persist in that new activity, in time you will be able to manage it with less and less stress. The body is adapting to the new demand which at first was an overload but with repetition becomes normal. So it is with training.

To be effective, the training exercise must overload the particular body system you want to train. If you continue with the same intensity and duration of exercise, the body will adapt to it. To maintain that level you will need to keep up with the exercise. If you stop or cut back significantly on the exercise, the body will re-adapt to the lower level. If you want to further increase your capability, you will have to increase the intensity and/or duration. Therefore, to train a 'system' you must 'overload' it sufficiently to promote adaptation but not so much that there is a breakdown of that system. By 'system' I mean a functional unit of the body, which may comprise a certain muscle group used, for example, to move an arm or a leg in a particular way or to maintain a balanced posture; it includes the nerve pathways controlling that muscle group and the bones and structures affected when the muscle group contracts.

Specificity

The adaptation resulting from an overload will be specific to the system overloaded. If you want strong fingers you will not get them by exercising your toes. But even that does not tell the whole story. The adaptation is specific not only to the system or muscle group involved but also to the way in which it is overloaded. The more precisely your training can replicate the sporting activity for which you are training, the bigger the gain in 'fitness' for that activity and the better the economy of training effort. If you want to train your arms for strength and endurance so that you can single sheet the main for the whole of both reaches in a force 5, it is an inefficient training effort to exercise with a sheet at an angle of say 45 degrees to the horizontal if, when racing, you will be working at 10 degrees. So 'specificity' in this context means that training must be specific to the system and to the activity for which you want to train.

Let us return to the qualified 'yes' in response to the question as to whether fitness can be achieved solely through sailing. Why do sailors find it almost impossible to get all the physical training they need for elite competition just by sailing? Suppose you are training for a world championship scheduled for August. So starting in January, you diligently spend every hour you can on the water. But the weather pattern that year is predominantly light winds with just the occasional force 3 to 4. When you get to the championship, perhaps in a different continent, the weather pattern is completely different with winds never less than force 4 for the whole competition. Will your body be adapted through your winter, spring and summer sailing, and no other training, to the demands of those conditions? You may be the world's best in racing tactics and boat handling in winds less than force 3, but if you haven't got a body specifically trained and adapted to the endurance and strength demands of hiking to windward and planing downwind in force 5, you will be hanging on just to survive as those 'fit for force 5' lap you on the second beat. The sailor therefore has a problem with 'training by doing' that others do not face.

In many sports, the athlete can train more intensively by setting himself targets of faster times. The sailor can only train harder by waiting for stronger winds, or travelling to areas where strong winds are common. For those who cannot afford to chase the winds, physical training is necessary for consistent good results in top competition, but it must be specific, it must be regular and it must be built up gradually to an intensity which represents an overload replicating the effects of the strongest winds in which you may race.

Specificity in training means two things:

- You must train the *specific* muscles you will use.
- These muscles must be trained *specifically* for the kind of activity they are going to perform.

A fitness programme consisting of jogging, squat-jumps and press-ups will do almost nothing for your ability to sit out and to pull on ropes, because it has not trained your stomach muscles at all. It has trained your thigh muscles to move but not to hold still, and it has trained the arm muscles involved in pushing but not those involved in pulling. This is not to say that such a programme is no use to anybody. For someone wanting to be a better jogger it is perfect. As a large part of the fitness training for a rugby forward it is very good. But for a dinghy racer it has the wrong specificity. This type of exercise can, however, figure in the programme, but it must not be the major feature.

The physiology of sailing

The physiology of sailing, or how the body works when we sail, has been a closed book until recent years.

In 1980 Prof Marchetti and colleagues in Rome compared the response of the heart to the stress of two sailing positions: hiking and trapezing. They found that the heart was beating much faster for the hiker than for the wire man, and that the blood pressure was also higher. By using sensors on the muscles, they discovered that the muscles on the front of the body of the hiker were working hard while those of the trapezer were only active in supporting the neck and in keeping both the calf/ankle stable.

The high pulse rates in hiking are required because the muscles are contracting isometrically. That is they are tightening up hard to hold the body in the required position and are neither shortening nor lengthening as they do so. When a muscle tightens hard in this way, it becomes so tight that it squashes the blood vessels and prevents the circulation from functioning properly. The muscle becomes starved of oxygen (ischaemia) and as a result, the contracting muscle begins to hurt. Having no proper blood supply, the working muscle can no longer obtain energy by the usual 'aerobic' method and has to work without oxygen, or anaerobically. As a result lactic acid begins to accumulate rapidly.

When the quads in the front of the thigh and the abdominal muscles become too painful, we have to sit inboard on the side tanks of the dinghy to rest while the circulation is restored. In contrast, during conventional endurance running sports, the high heart rate is associated with high oxygen consumption as the muscles work hard aerobically to sustain performance. They are, of course, contracting and relaxing and so allow a good blood circulation.

The more oxygen available within the body, the better the performance. Indeed as the measure of potential maximum performance in endurance sports the Max VO_2 (which is a measure of the maximum oxygen uptake that the body can manage to reach) became the key test. Also, oxygen uptake is closely related to the heart rate in a linear fashion, so that it is possible in testing fitness to predict the Max VO_2 from the theoretical maximum heart rate.

Our theoretical maximum heart rate is obtained by subtracting our age in years from 220. Thus a 40-year-old man would have a likely maximum heart rate of 220−40=180. A man of 60, a maximum of 160. We perform less well in sport as we get older because we can no longer hit high rates, and so we carry less oxygen to our muscles where they use it to burn the fuel with which the muscle works.

About ten years ago, two dinghy sailing physiologists, Voglatzis and Spurway, working in Glasgow measured dinghy sailors on the water with expensive portable gas analysis equipment. They have shown that hiking dinghy sailors may have high pulse rates, but *unlike* the endurance runners these high rates are *not* associated with high oxygen consumption.

This important finding turns on its head some of the previous ideas about the best way to train for dinghy sailing. We used to say that since the heart rates were as high in dinghy sailing as in running we should train our hearts in the same way. Therefore, general aerobic type fitness training was advised with the addition of specific exercises for local body strength. Does this approach still apply?

The answer is that for the very average unfit or inactive adult there is much to be gained from a fitness programme of the old type, partly because not all of sailing is in the form of crunching beats. There is some 'down hill' work, and there are many times when the quads and abs are not contracting isometrically. Every time the sailor adjusts his position he either shortens or elongates his muscles. The particular muscle ceases to act isometrically, and at once some fresh blood enters the muscle so that it can resume aerobic metabolism again. The pain goes until the next episode of sustained isometric contraction.

But for the high flyer, training takes on an added dimension, for there is now another way to train. In an isometrically contracting muscle, the circulation of blood is obstructed less when it is not contracting as hard as it is when it is maximally contracted. The aim now is to try to develop the muscle so that it is strong enough to hold the hiking position when working at less than 100 per cent maximal contraction. If we can improve the muscle so that the body position is maintained at say 40 per cent of the maximal contraction we get the best of both worlds. We have a muscle working hard enough isometrically to hold our hiking position, but with an oxygen supply that is adequate for its needs, so we do not have to come inboard to rest from pain.

The best way to improve this training requirement is by the use of the hiking bench – longer and longer spells on the bench, which should replicate the shape of the dinghy for which we are training (training is very specific as far as joint angles and stresses are concerned). Discomfort in the anterior abdominal muscles will be noticed first, but as these improve the discomfort may be more in the thigh.

Warning: Those who have unduly high blood pressure should avoid prolonged use of the hiking bench, since this is associated with a raising of the blood pressure. For the very top sailors, there is maybe less use for the hiking bench since many of the semi-pros or professionals are in their boats all the time these days. The dinghy itself is, after all, the ultimate in hiking-bench design. But if you don't want to go for a run on a filthy night how about an hour in front of the fire reading or watching the telly while sitting on your section of 505? Or why don't you offer to trapeze next season and ask your crew to drive the thing for a change?

In the sailing physiology world there is an academic north/south divide. On the one hand there may be too much emphasis upon aerobic endurance type preparation. On the other hand maybe the hiking bench is over emphasised. It could be that as an individual you try what mix is best for you. The canny northerners advise a training programme based upon isometric static lower body training on the hiking bench, coupled with dynamic upper body training of the arms and shoulders, since these are in constant motion while sailing in a breeze.

Planning a fitness programme

The first thing that a sailor (or any other sportsman) must think about when planning a fitness programme is his individual needs. These are very unlikely to be met by copying the training adopted (quite properly) for team games at school. Think first about the special requirements of the job you do on the boat. Here are some pointers.

- Are you a dinghy helm or a crew in a non-trapeze dinghy? If so, your emphasis must be on hiking endurance and on armwork.

- Are you a trapeze crew? Then speed and agility (arm and leg) will be at a premium, and abdominal muscle endurance will matter much less.
- Are you a winch-man? If so, all your specific concentration must be on arm-power.

However much you want to improve your fitness for your particular role, you must also ask yourself another set of questions: what are your personal strengths and weaknesses? Some are obvious: if you are a 90kg trapezer you almost certainly have strength to spare, but should work on agility and try to lose some weight at the same time. The converse applies if you are 65kg and want to campaign a Finn. To be a bit more specific, do you sit out your 470 fairly well, but lack the arm strength to hoist that kite fast when it is blowing a hoolie? Do you hang pretty far out from your Laser, even on the final beat, but come in more slowly than you should in quick tacks and unexpected lulls?

Questions like these are hard to answer honestly, because they mean you are going to have to work most at the things you are worst at – whereas it is far more comfortable to go on training at (and possibly even boasting about) those parts of your role which come more easily. So check your self-assessment with your sailing coach, your crew or another racer who knows you well. They may know nothing about fitness training, yet they will be able to spot your deficiencies better than you can.

Include some generality

This section began by emphasising the need for specific training because 90 per cent of people who try to train without professional advice adopt a programme which is insufficiently specific. On the other hand, the professional adviser would always include some non-specific (ie general) training in a programme. There are two reasons:

- If you strengthen only the muscles required for your principal actions you will become unbalanced. This does not just look unsightly; it can cause injury. For in sudden movement the strong muscles may tear the weak ones, or strain the structure which is receiving an unbalanced pull.
- There are two systems of the body upon which every sort of exercise puts demands, and which must be conditioned first before embarking upon a strenuous specificity-emphasising regime. These are the heart (plus the rest of the circulatory system) and the lungs (plus other components of the respiratory system).

A well-designed training programme, if you are starting from scratch (following perhaps either an after-season lay-off, or a season which had involved too much long-distance travel) might at first have you devoting 80 or even 100 per cent of effort to the recovery of general fitness. Even in the last intensive period before your major event of the year you should put 20 to 30 per cent of effort in this direction. Hence it is valid to say that the jog/jump/press-up programme which contributes to general, though not specific, fitness would only modestly help your hiking endurance – rather than do no good at all!

Build generality into endurance, into strength, into speed

Work out how long a training period you have before the competition starts in earnest. Let us assume it is somewhere between 12 and 24 weeks. Divide this into four roughly equal periods, of approximately three to six weeks each. Then assuming you are a healthy, young (or youngish!) adult, develop your programme thus:

1 *In the first phase build general fitness.* The jog/jump/press-up kind of routine would be all right here, though proper circuit-training two or three times a week would be better. Other sports such as cycling or swimming are very worth while, and have particular advantages if you are one of those whose knees or ankles do not take kindly to road-running. Racquet games also introduce variety with negligible risk of injury. *But remember that if you are over 30 you get fit to play squash rather than play squash to get fit. Over 40 this is even more important.* During this period, light work at your specific needs will be useful. However, it is quite acceptable to leave this out if you prefer something new at this stage, in order to reduce the psychological problem of boredom later on.

2 *In the second phase build specific endurance.* Specific exercises must begin at the start of this period if they have not been done before. These are the exercises which match your particular sailing role, such as abdominal exercises for hiking – specific suggestions are made later. Do not give up the general fitness training, but gradually increase the time spent on specifics, paring down on the general exercise to make room. However, in this period neither forces nor speeds greater than you can easily manage should be attempted. The aim by the end of this second phase of about six weeks is merely to be able to do the exercises easily for quite long periods.

Up to this point the training programme is safe for sailors of any age. Girls under 15, boys under 16, and adults over 40-45 years who have not kept up hard physical activity during their mature lives should extend phase (2) indefinitely and not go on to phases (3) and (4).

3 *In the third phase adults and young sailors who have stopped growing may build specific strength.* Begin now to increase the loads in your specific strength exercises – initially perhaps twice a week, and then later in every session. If you are hiking, or lifting bodyweight, add to it with a weight jacket or a part-filled rucksack. Some general training should still be done in this phase, but on all but one or two days per week it should now be confined to the warm-up and round-off periods with specific strength exercises as the core of the training session.

4 *In the fourth phase add specific speed.* In this final period, some of each of the previous activities are still undertaken but speedwork is added, first to two specific training sessions, then to all of them. For speedwork reduce the load (eg go back to unaugmented body weight) and strive to increase your speed. Do repetition sit-ups, rope pulls (or whatever) against the clock, and set yourself targets for small but definite improvements each week. This new feature must be placed near the start of each training session, because fatigue makes speed-improvement impossible. Later in each workout you will be adding yet further to endurance, but not speed.

Finally, take at least three days of rest before each major series. Light general training can be done in this period, but not the hard stuff. You will have gained nothing if you go into a big event with those specific muscle groups fatigued. Training (normally of phase 4 type) should be resumed between major series, but always with three to four days' lay-off before the next big event starts.

All increases of effort must be gradual

First, increase the frequency of training. Start the general fitness programme with three to four sessions a week, then increase to five then to six. But even in the final strength and speed phases, do not exceed that. A day or two off per week is necessary, to allow time for recovery from minor strains and sheer fatigue. Remember that the adaptation to the stimulus of training takes place between training sessions not during training – there must be time for adaptation otherwise there is no point in training!

Next, increase duration. Increase the lengths of runs, and the number of repetitions of strength exercises, as fitness builds, but cut back on duration for the first three to four times after every increase of load or speed. In phase 4, speed increases must be gradual. If you are really trying in the first place, improvements by more than a few per cent will be unusual.

Quoting actual figures for any of these aspects, except those of safety, is a doubtful practice. Individual capabilities differ so much that you are probably better to assess yourself and set your own goals. But the sort of goals that might be reasonable would be to:

- Increase the duration of runs from 20 to 30 minutes during the general-fitness stage.
- Increase the repetitions of unloaded sit-ups from 20 at the start of the second stage to 50 at the end of the third.
- Increase the maximum weight that can be lifted via a pulley from 30 to 37kg in 12 weeks.

Remember always that much smaller increases should be expected in strength and speed than in endurance.

Never attempt exercise without a warm-up

To do so is to court injury. A three-minute jog and a further three to four minutes of exercises from the general fitness programme, used as preparation for the strenuous workout, will get the heart and lungs going and the blood flowing fast through the muscles and connective tissues. They will also, quite literally, raise the temperature within the muscles. All these factors are highly desirable before the stressful training start. In the warm-up be sure to include light, loose activity for the muscles you are going to impose real loads on later, eg two sets of six or so non-pressurised sit-ups should be part of the sequence before you go on to a hiking bench. Also include some stretching exercises for the neck shoulders, back, hamstrings and quads between the warm-up and the hard work of the day – but remember to stretch slowly and not to 'bounce'. Take a tip – warm up and stretch in the same way before each race as well.

Specific sailing exercises

Only suggestions can be given here – take them as illustrations of principles rather than as prescriptions from which you must not depart. It is assumed throughout that you are training at home: a well-equipped gym provides more scope for many types of training, though not necessarily for all. For general fitness for sailing, sit-ups, press-ups, pull-ups, burpees, star jumps, squat thrusts and side bends are all worthwhile exercises.

Training for sitting out

The abdominal (stomach) muscles, the quadriceps (upper thighs) and the ilio-psoas (a muscle rising in the pelvis and lower back and passing to the thigh bone) take the main strain here. Much of it is static (technically 'isometric') strain, but you must also be able to move in again quickly – and your arms must be able to pull hard on ropes while you are out there.

A hiking bench is best. But make sure it matches your boat really closely. It is pointless, during training, to be supported at mid-thigh if in reality the gunwhale of your boat supports you behind the knees. Also make sure that the bench is either well rounded or well padded, or both – you can do lasting damage if you cut off the circulation at the backs of your legs during every training session. Nevertheless, with these provisos in mind, it is possible to construct very good makeshift benches from suitably positioned furniture – like dining chairs laid on their backs with 'toestraps' round their feet, or the arms of sofas brought near to heavy tables. When the boat simulation is right, get so used to the bench that you can read a book in your standard 'force 5 position'. Build up from just five or so little hikes lasting only one to two minutes each to three or four hikes lasting 10 minutes each. Do 10 repetitions, once or twice in each hike, of coming in sharply and at once going out again. Also try rotating yourself to right and left while you are out there, as you would do many times on a real boat.

Throughout all this, remember that there is a vital rule when hiking a dinghy. In extending your upper body over the water to obtain greater leverage, when going to windward or when reaching, the body should pivot outboard from the hips. Undue forward curvature of the lumbar spine, caused by hollowing the lower back, causes

Stretching exercises

Golden rules

1 Stretch is an important part of 'warm up' and 'warm down'. Warm up *before* stretching.

2 Never stretch cold muscles. Do a five-minute gentle jog in tracksuit or warm clothing.

3 Never bounce when stretching – this may cause injury.

4 Never hold your breath while stretching.

5 Hold the stretched position so that you can feel the stretch but not be in pain.

Stretching the back of the thigh (hamstrings)

You may do this either standing with the leg placed on a table or desk top; or by sitting on a bench, desk or table top with the leg to be stretched lifted up onto the raised surface.

Keep your leg to be stretched straight at the knee and lean forward until you feel the muscle at the back of your thigh stretch. Do not try to touch your toes or to put your head on your knees because this exercise is not to stretch your back. Try instead to think of putting your 'belly' on the top of your thigh.

Hold the position of stretch for 10 seconds. Then relax for 2 seconds before you hold the stretch again for a further 10 seconds. Relax for 2 seconds and hold for a final 10 seconds. You will probably notice that you go further after each 10-second stretch. You are not to go from stretched to painful to very painful. A feeling of stretch is all you require.

Stretching the front of the thigh (quadriceps)

While standing up, bend the leg to be stretched up behind you and grasp the ankle with the hand of the same side of the body. Pull with the hand until you feel the stretch in the front of the thigh. You can do this wrongly if you do not ensure that your thigh is directly in line with your body. This is because one of the four 'quads' muscles arises from the pelvis and is thus less stretched if the hip is bent. If you bend the hip you stretch only three of the four 'quads' muscles. Hold the stretched position for 30 seconds, broken into 10-second segments as for the 'hams'.

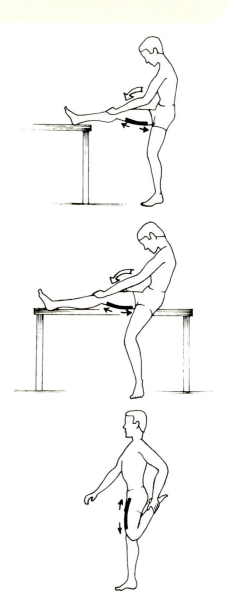

Stretching the calf muscle at the back of the lower leg

Face the wall with the leg to be stretched well behind you. Keep the heel on the floor and the foot pointing directly at the wall. With the knee straight lean towards the wall controlling your position with your hands on the wall at shoulder height with elbows bent. The other leg is placed closer to the wall with the knee bent to help to control the position. As you lean towards the wall you will feel your calf muscles stretching. Hold the position for 30 seconds as above. Then, maintaining the position, bend the rear knee, sink towards the floor until you again feel a stretch deeper in the calf.

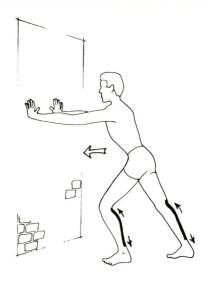

Improving the stomach or abdominal muscles (abs)

Lie on your back on the floor with bent knees. Make sure your pelvis is tilted so that your lower back is pushed into the floor. Feel with your hand to see that you are doing this properly. Hollow your abdomen by trying to pull your navel inwards. You may have to practise your pelvic tilting and abdominal hollowing separately before you are able to do the exercise properly since these two positions are an integral part of the exercise. Now place your hands on your ears (not behind the neck) and slowly lift head and shoulders with your chin tucked in to look between your knees. There is no need to come up to a sitting position. Hold the position for a slow count of five, breathing normally as you do so.

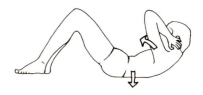

Stretching the ilio-psoas muscle (a powerful hiking muscle)

Adopt the position shown in the diagram with one leg placed well in front with the knee bent and the other almost as far behind as it will go (feet facing forward). You may either balance in this position or place the hands upon the floor. Move the pelvis forwards and down towards the ground and you will feel a stretch in front of the upper thigh and groin of the backward leg. Do not bounce. Hold the stretch for 30 seconds as above.

undue sheering stress upon some lumbar discs and compression of others. In such a position, rotation or sideways tilting of the spine when helming or pulling sheets may prove the last straw to a suspect, ageing or immature spine. The penalty is likely to be pain in your lower back for the rest of your life because the wrong muscles have been loaded and the bottom vertebrae compressed. The best posture is to keep your legs bent. However, shallow hulls, like those of Lasers, impose straight legs. **Keep your back curled, whatever your boat.**

If you do not have a bench for exercising, do bent-leg sit-ups with your feet flat on the floor and your hands on your ears. Do them in the 'trunk-curl' fashion, lifting your head off the floor first, then your shoulders, then your back – avoid a hollow back, for the same reason as in hiking. Do 10 such movements then stay with your back just clear of the floor for 10 to 20 seconds, then do the trunk-curls again. If your feet are flat on the floor you are exercising your anterior abdominal muscles. If you repeat the exercise with your feet under a restraining bar you are also exercising the ilio-psoas, the powerful hiking muscle of the pelvis. Take a short rest and repeat the set. Do, say, two sets of 20 curls each, building up to four sets of 40 or 50 by the end. In addition, train your quadriceps on a leg extension bench – the kind where you straighten your leg against a weight. Or do the one-legged squat thrusts – just 5 with each leg at first, building up to 3 or 4 sets of 8 to 10 thrusts each.

Finally there is a quadriceps exercise which you can do as you stand in a queue. With your legs absolutely straight, brace hard one leg at a time making the thigh muscles stand out just above the knee; hold for 5 seconds then relax. Brace alternate legs, say, 6 to 8 times each, 15 to 20 times a day. People may look a little curiously at your expression, but you will be considerably less likely to suffer knee pain after strong-wind races the following summer.

Major abdominal strengthening is an instance where counterbalancing development (of the back) requires specific exercise also. Do this by the prone lift: lie on your stomach, and slowly raise either the feet or the torso off the floor. Hold for 5 seconds, lower and repeat 5 to 10 times. Do not lift both ends at once into a 'banana' position.

Training for sheeting in

Pull-ups on wall-bars, doors or wardrobes are useful; they strengthen the pulling muscles of the upper arms and chest. However, they will not enhance your grip on a rope. Much better, therefore, is to do your pull-ups on a tail of rope. Most people can find a tree, banister or garage rafter from which to hang one. However, even here the angle of pull is unrealistic.

Lifting weights on ropes represents the effort better. If you can arrange a pulley so that the rope leads up to your waist at a 30–45° angle, this exercise will be pretty specific, even to the correct lead angle. By doing both this and the pull-ups you will be a great deal stronger in 12 to 18 weeks.

Having got that far with your equipment, though, maybe you can position the pulley to enable you to add simultaneous arm exercise to your periods on the hiking bench. Then you really will be in business! Two alternative positions are necessary: one for left arm (port tack) training and one for right arm (starboard tack) training. Since these positions will be at floor level, you need a second block higher up if you are going to lift a weight. So it may be easier to work against a spring or bungee cord on the hiking bench/frame. On the other hand, weights are more easily adjustable as you get stronger, eg bricks in a bucket.

Whichever kind of load you choose, *strong fastenings* of mechanical parts to the frame are essential. Incidentally, if hand tiredness is a limitation to your performance in hard weather, try putting a rubber ball in each pocket and kneading it as you go about your daily business. A few months of this can make a surprising difference – and does not even count as 'training time' at all.

Training for trapeze work

Many trapezers suffer not only fatigue during races but back pain off the water. Unfortunately the exact problem seems to vary with the individual and his particular harness. The best general advice is that a good deal of trunk exercise is worth while – but in this case treat abdomen and back equally. Trunk twists, side-bends and toe-touching are all *specific* exercises for the trapeze sailor but, just as when they are used in association with a warm-up, do them *slowly*, don't try to get further by momentum. 'Ballistic stretching', as this is called, is much more likely to cause injury. If twisting and tilting the spine is uncomfortable, *do not do it*!

Do a good number of prone lifts, aiming to cope with three sets of 10 by the end of three or four months. Include some trunk-curls but only a quarter as many as if you were hike-training. Regard press-ups here as a specific exercise, not for the arms but for the trunk – keep your body straight, or your rear end very slightly high; don't let your body sag. Wall-bar exercises are useful trunk strengtheners too, if you can find a rafter or branch to do them from. In particular the hanging leg-raise; as you hang from a bar, raise your thighs (with bent knees) until they are horizontal in front of you, hold for three seconds and then lower; then repeat five times. As you get stronger, gradually extend your lower legs until they are straight out too – it is much harder! If you have ever found your legs getting tired in a long hard-weather race, then leg-thrusts will help; squat jumps and/or burpees should make a real contribution to your training. Sheeting-in exercises are also wholly appropriate to the trapezer.

Training for the winch-man

Few winch-men are total specialists, so general circuit training and the rope-pull exercises suggested above should figure substantially in the programme. Leg raises and pull-ups on bars (which are much more like winch handles than ropes) plus press-ups and some punch-bag training are also appropriate. Better still is 'sawing' with a partner of comparable strength, if available. However, none of these exercises will train your arms specifically for rotational movements, so see if you can find an old hand-cranked grindstone and arrange to rotate it against the braking influence of, say, a wedge of wood. Or rig a bike so that you work the pedals by hand against the brakes, or against an adjustable-tension resistance belt bearing upon the rim. If your winch is a vertical 'coffee grinder', then try to set up your simulators to match; if it is the more usual horizontal action, try to mount the bike or grindstone on its side.

Weight training

Weight training is a potential hazard – an 80kg athlete lifting 90kg overhead in an incorrect way can exert a force of 900kg across the lumbar spine. Yet someone who does no heavy work can suffer from chronic backache because of long periods of standing at work, perhaps exacerbated by unequal leg length causing a lateral tilt of the spine.

The following points about avoiding back injury during weight training should be considered:

1   Weight training by children is not appropriate and caution should be used for growing youths. This is because certain back conditions can be made considerably worse by such training. In youth sailing, careful thought should be given to the likely eventual build of the young sailor by a study of his mother, father, brothers and sisters.

2   Weight training may entail the use of a multigym where a sailor may train alone, or by using his own body weight in training movements. Training with free weights requires caution and training partners. Such weight training should be undertaken in groups of three, if heavy free weights on a bar are being used. This is because of the risk of losing control of the weight, with the consequent leverage causing significant injury to back or shoulder. One person should stand either side of the lifter to take immediate charge in the event of a failed lift. The use of a pair of stands with forked tops upon which to lower the bar is absolutely necessary if training alone. For fitness and stamina, the use of fast repetitions of light weights is required. For muscle bulking, the weights should be heavier.

Weight training is difficult to understand if one thinks in terms of heavy and light weights. One sailor's heavy weight is another's light weight. For this reason we have to think of the weight as it applies to one person only. We do this by defining the weight in terms of how difficult it is for a given person to lift it. The definition is in terms of RM or Repetitions Maximum. One RM is the heaviest weight we can lift once only 'in good form'. That is, it is a weight that is too heavy for us to lift a second time. In lifting it once only we do so in a controlled and non-dangerous way.

A five RM weight becomes one that we can lift five times in succession in good style but which is too heavy for us to lift six times yet lighter than the weight that we could only lift four times. The accent has to be on the 'in good form' so that we do not injure ourselves with the last lift.

On this scale, one person's 5 RM weight may be half of another's, but both sailors know what degree of heaviness we are talking about if we say go and train with weight equivalent to 5 RM. In training for general fitness with weights we are thinking of weights of 10 RM or over (ie 10 RM weight or less, say 12 or 20 RM). In such training it is conventional to lift 15 RM, for example, in a fairly rapid sequence, repeating the sequence several times.

In weight training for muscle bulking, the weight limit is from 10 RM or less (10 RM weight or heavier). In this form of training the weight-lifting sequence may be in steadily increasing degree of heaviness. That is from perhaps 10 RM weight to 8 RM to 6 RM; progressively to 4, 3, 2 and finally 1 RM. This being the heaviest weight that the sailor can manage to lift once in good form. It is usual to work upwards in weight, lifting more each time. If you start by lifting your 1 RM maximum, you may not be in good enough shape to progress downwards in weight!

Of course to determine your RM you have to try a maximum lift to start with. *Don't be too ambitious. Do not injure yourself. Do the lifts under supervision.* If your selected 1 RM maximum is in fact 3 RM there is no problem; as you improve, your RM will have to be re-adjusted anyway. At the end of three months' training, it is likely that you will be lifting a lot more than on the first week. This is partly due to the acquisition of skill in the task, partly to your learning to recruit more muscle fibres in a given muscle during the lift, and partly due to your having achieved your aim of making a stronger and more bulky muscle. Thus every few weeks both heavyweight and lightweight trainers have to redefine their RM so that they are still on the effective side of the dividing line for their chosen weight-training routine.

Balanced training

Remember that every muscle has an 'opposite number' which is the muscle which works against the one you are training. If you seek to build up your quads on the front of the thigh, which are the extenders of the knee joint, remember the hamstrings which, at the back of the thigh, act as knee flexors. If the hams fall more than 60 per cent behind the quads in strength, there is every chance that you will 'pull' a hamstring muscle. This same logic will apply to all muscle groups. Sailing in a dinghy is very much a sport which places stress upon (and thus develops) muscles on the front of the body. The sailing position in the semi-hike is interesting in that if a photo of the sailor is rotated 90 degrees so that the feet are on the ground, as opposed to being in mid-air hanging on the straps, the posture is that of a bent old man or woman walking with the aid of a stick (tiller extension)!

When devising your muscle training programme, therefore, think in terms of a balanced development. Also, make sure that you stretch these wonderful new muscle fibres that have been so hard won, since a well-stretched developed muscle will be of more use to you than one which is so tense that the joint which it controls now has a limited range of movement.

Lightweight fast repetitions tend not to increase muscle bulk, but will improve muscle tone and capillary circulation so that the blood supply improves, and the muscles are more efficient. Heavyweight training and prolonged isometric work will produce a more bulky muscle which is more powerful. It has been suggested, however, that this results in a bulky heart muscle and raises blood pressure.

Common sailing injuries and their prevention

Competitive water sports are the cause of few injuries overall – less than two per cent in one study at an inland hospital. However, unaccustomed exercise is said to be occasionally fatal, frequently injurious and always painful!

Skill is paramount in safety. This involves physical control, an ability to read the situation, assess risk and know how to offset it and to be able to take necessary action. Sailors must, therefore, develop effective and efficient movement patterns, which should become conditioned reflexes.

The sailor is made vulnerable by fatigue and by nervous tension. The beginner or unskilled is especially open to injury both to himself and to other people. In addition, skill will not protect against conditions arising from overexertion if the sailor pushes himself beyond the protection afforded by his own level of fitness.

Causes of sailing injuries

A survey of sailing injuries in the UK by Dr Newton printed in *The Physician* (August 1984) showed the following injuries: the back, 35 per cent; head, 25 per cent; knees, 20 per cent; shoulders, 4 per cent and finally elbows, 5 per cent. The ankle is not prone to frequent injury in sailing due to the fact that the leg is not in motion as often, or as violently, as in some sports.

In terms of treatment, there is nothing specific to a sailing injury that makes it different when it has occurred to the same injury sustained in another sport or in a domestic or road accident.

Sports injuries occur more frequently both at the start of the competitive season, when the athlete is unfit, and at the end of the season when the athlete is tired after a long period of competition. In sailing, the time for injury may be the annual class

Make sure you are wearing the right clothing for the weather conditions, so that you always maintain the correct body temperature.

championships spread over a week of tiring, back-to-back competition, combined with a social programme which may damage coordination and lead to injury. In a single race, the time of greatest risk is at the start – before the athlete is properly warmed, particularly muscle elasticity, and near the end of a race when the muscles are fatigued by an accumulation of waste products that inhibit normal function, and particularly in sailing, by cold and ischaemia (poor circulation).

Optimum conditions are needed for effective body function be this internal (for example digestion) or musculo-skeletal for movement. The body core temperature is maintained within narrow limits and muscular contraction and relaxation in response to a command from the brain will be faster and more complete if the muscle is at the correct temperature. Having contracted, the muscle will relax in preparation for the next contraction at a faster rate if warmed up, than if it is cold.

Taking two opposing muscle groups: if one is cold and one is warm, there is a risk of an uncoordinated contraction which may cause muscle injury. The rate of recovery of a fatigued muscle will depend upon blood circulation, temperature and supply of correct nutritional factors from the blood. This in turn requires the right food input at the correct time and in adequate quantity.

Muscle tissue itself varies in type for different tasks in the body. For example in a chicken, which mainly walks or runs, we find darker muscle fibres in the legs, and pale meat in the breast, whereas in the pheasant, the 'fast' contracting flying muscles of the breast are dark fibres. The particular fibre mix in each individual is ordained by his or her genes. It follows that it is not always possible to make oneself a champion in certain sports unless the right muscle configuration has been inherited! However, in a sport like sailing, this should not prevent the well trained from reaching the top.

The available range of movement is an important factor in injury. In body contact sports, like rugby, wrestling or American football, the risk to a limb or joint is considerable, if full flexion and extension are limited. The risk in sailing is not so great but the ability to sail may well be greatly reduced if the sailor has a limited range of movement. Factors limiting the range of movement include:

- Age, with early osteo-arthritic joint changes.
- Pre-existing injury with old scar tissue in muscles.
- Restrictive clothing, wet suits, life jackets and trapeze harness which limit full movement.
- Available room in the boat, eg boom clearance.

Avoiding injuries to the lower back

The lumbar spine is one of nature's grey areas. There seems to have been no set human design; there are a number of recognised variables. It does not follow, however, that a back with an unusual configuration is a painful or unstable back, and it certainly does not follow that if a lumbar spine is seen on an X-ray to be normal, it will be trouble free. X-rays show only bone structures; the trouble often lies in the associated discs, ligaments and joints.

Pain is the key word in relation to back problems. Back pain may be accompanied by pain extending to the buttocks or down the thigh, often as far as the calf or foot. There may be loss of tendon reflex, loss of sensation of touch, pins and needles sensations and significant wasting of muscle bulk. A sailor with such symptoms should not be allowed to sail until passed fit. These symptoms are caused by pressure on a spinal nerve or nerve root. Undue flexion, extension, rotation or tilt of the spine may increase this effect.

The use of the weight jacket should not be encouraged and its use is now prohibited in youth sailing. Loading of the spine produces 'creep effects' – the spine stiffens and is less capable of absorbing shocks. Compression of the spine can cause damage to discs and can even cause you to shrink! Loss of vertebral height has been recorded in healthy young adult males after loading the shoulders for 20 minutes with only 9kg (Fitzgerald 1972). Creep effects are accelerated if the loaded spine is then exposed to vibration, known as the 'Vibro Creep Phenomenon'.

Conditioning factors making back injury more likely are a prolonged state of static loading, vibratory stress, repetitive impacts and shocks. Individual capacity for spinal stress varies greatly depending upon size and physical characteristics of the vertebral column, muscular strength and skill, and on the presence or absence of degenerative changes and other abnormalities.

People suffering from chronic low back pain need to learn how to lift properly using their legs and avoiding strain on the back. This means being careful when launching and recovering a dinghy. Also, when hauling on sheets in the boat, it is possible to help preserve the back by extending the legs to assist pulling. A firm bed for sleeping, correct car seating and correct sitting posture also help. Frequently, pain in the lower back is associated with tight hamstring muscles, so stretching these can be beneficial.

Certain low spine problems are caused by undue mobility of the lumbar vertebrae, which enables them to slip forward, thus trapping the nerves. Such conditions may be helped by a supporting belt or corset. A neoprene belt worn when sailing should be worn over other clothing and have velcro adjustment.

Scheuermann's disease is a common condition caused by a growth disturbance occurring in the adolescent spine. In this condition the back is often noticeably rounded. Undue flexion of the back during growth is to be avoided if there is pain associated with such rounding. Careful choice of boat may be of help – choose one which your body weight can handle in the mid-upper wind range. Playing in the second row of the scrum is not advised either!

Neck injuries

The cervical spine (neck area) is a very mobile portion of the back and the head is a very heavy organ. The neck often shows signs of undue early wear and tear, or damage from injury in other sports or accidents. Pain from the neck may extend down the arms. Older sailors with neck problems may find difficulty in scanning the water, looking up to the rig, telltales or masthead indicators.

Head injuries

It may seem obvious that head injuries should have been near the top of the list in the survey. However, to those injured, the mechanism of injury is not always that obvious. In sailing the call of 'lee oh' or 'gybe oh' is used as a warning. This call is often not used by a practised crew sailing together all the time, and a newcomer may be caught unawares and hit on the head. Particular care must be taken, therefore, in coaching those who are hard of hearing or who are deaf or blind. Helmets are seldom used in sailing but regularly in canoeing. They should be considered for windsurfers, for learner dinghy sailors and for those who have had a previous head injury. Some would say that they are worthwhile protection for all sailors who have the courage to wear them! The plastic type is inexpensive, adjusts to several sizes, and is light in weight.

In the event of a head injury, the coach should insist that the sailor takes no part in further sailing that day, as delayed onset of unconsciousness is not uncommon. The coach must be confident in resuscitation techniques and make sure that an airway is an essential part of his equipment. Remember that if a blow is hard enough to render a sailor unconscious, it may also have caused significant injury to the cervical spine. If the sailor is paralysed from the neck down and can't talk, then both sailor and coach are in serious trouble.

Knee injuries

The knee is potentially an unstable joint. To function properly, it requires good muscle tone in groups of muscles that cross the joint from above to below and vice versa. These pull the thigh bone (femur) and the shin bone (tibia) hard against each other, compressing the cartilages, which act as shims, between them. Angularity sideways is prevented by the inner (medial) ligament and the outer (lateral) ligament. Fore and aft movement is restricted by the cruciate ligaments inside the joint. They all work as a team.

Loss of function of part of the system can result in an unstable knee, which will rapidly become a painful, injured knee. It follows that, at all times, the muscles must be maintained in good tone with good bulk, and be well stretched. In the event of a knee injury, a swelling of the joint occurring a day or so after the event probably indicates that fluid has seeped from bruised tissues. Rapid swelling within an hour or so may indicate bleeding within the joint. If bleeding is suspected, an immediate hospital opinion is essential as 75 per cent of such cases have significant damage to internal structures.

Anterior knee pain

Some people suffer from pain behind the kneecap caused by its roughened under-surface grinding against the articular surface of the lower femur. This condition is found in those whose knees hyper-extend, and is common in children. During exercise with the knee bent, it has been suggested that a force as much as 10 times body weight may be applied through the knee. The stability of this joint will vary according to its degree of flexion.

In traditional hiking, as in the Finn dinghy, the (medial) inner quadriceps muscle is 'resting', while the main bulk of the other three quads is in sustained isometric contraction, therefore developing into a very strong muscle, which alters the dynamics of the joint. Anterior knee pain may become worse. In the Laser, the sustained, almost straight leg sailing will develop the medial quads and improve the condition. A third of the youth squad in winter training have this problem. After six weeks of isometric medial quads exercise, this is greatly reduced.

Ankle injuries

The ankle has not significantly featured as a structure in sailing injuries. It is not often injured in sailing but it is often injured in other activities that the sailor will be doing in training for sailing. The most common of the injuries is the inversion sprain when the foot is turned inwards awkwardly while it is carrying body weight. As a consequence, the ligaments on the outer side of the ankle joint are damaged. Swelling and bruising will occur, and on occasion the bone on one side or other of the joint may be fractured.

In the case of the sprain it is quite likely that the sailor will be advised to rest the part for too long. Too much rest may cause vital 'proprioceptive' function to be lost. This function keeps us aware of the position of our body in space, so that we may automatically make correct postural adjustments at once. Incorrect adjustment of the position of the ankle results in further injury. Practice with a 'wobble board' should start within 36 hours of the average ankle sprain, after observation of the ritual of initial ice, rest, compression and elevation (RICE). This rule also applies after a knee injury. As a substitute for the wobble board try a thick off-cut of upholstery foam, stand on it on the sprained ankle and swing the good leg slowly in all directions until the ankle feels secure.

The design of training shoes leaves much to be desired and helps cause ankle problems. High heel tabs found on most trainers are a cause of a soreness (peritendonitis) of the Achilles tendon which can rapidly become a chronic condition. Frequent physiotherapy without changing shoes is expensive and injurious to the tissues. Rugby boots, cricket boots and basketball boots may also cause similar problems.

Other injuries

Overuse injuries, like tennis and golfer's elbow, are caused by poor technique. Over-gripping the tiller handle or the use of too small or too large a handle may cause problems. The grip should be light but firm. In boardsailing, pain in the forearm can be caused by too tight a grip upon the boom. Some top board sailors have suffered from compartmental compression of the circulation to forearm muscles, due to excessive development of these muscles within a limited space.

Many sailors in top competition take up running as part of their training and most find themselves running on road surfaces. Unlike athletes of the running world, they may not possess a good running gait, and if heavy-footed, may develop stress fractures. These may be prevented by the use of Sorbothane running shoe insoles made of a special compound which dissipates the force of impact in various directions, reducing the likelihood of stress fractures. They are available from good sport shops.

Gloves and suitable clothing are mandatory, particularly during winter training. Head covering greatly reduces heat loss. During cold winter training in Ireland, the grip strength of ten Laser sailors was recorded before and after a one-hour session on the water. A loss of up to 40 per cent grip strength was noted in all but one sailor – the only girl. Females have better insulation than males due to thicker fat layers in the skin. It is very important not to suffer from hypothermia as it can result in loss of both physical and mental functions. Wearing the correct clothing is vital to prevent this from occurring. Coaches should watch out for the signs (eg shivering, confusion and a slow pulse), particularly in younger or older age groups after a capsize.

Risks to sailors

1   Tetanus It is advised that sailors be protected against tetanus which regularly causes death in the UK.

2   Weil's disease This is a virus spread by the urine of infected rats. The risk is greatest in fresh water but can occur in the partly salty waters of estuaries. The virus enters the body through cuts, blisters and throat membranes. Wounds should be thoroughly washed and protected with fresh waterproof dressings. The disease starts as an illness with symptoms rather like 'flu', but jaundice may occur. All who sail where there is a known rat population should be warned to tell their doctors of the risk, if reporting sick with a flu-like illness. Weil's disease is a medical emergency not to be treated over the phone with advice to take 'a couple of aspirin and two days in bed'. But unless advised of your sporting interest and risk, your doctor may reasonably assume if 'flu' is about that this is the cause of your illness.

3   Sore throats and fevers No athlete should be physically active when unwell for fear of the heart muscle being affected.

Psychology of the injury-prone athlete

The anxiety-prone athlete is also a loser in the sense of being more injury-prone. Some athletes find competitive sport so anxiety-inducing that they try to get over this by meeting it head on. Being overtly aggressive and fearless, such people tempt fate by testing their indestructibility, making them more prone to injury. They are attracted to high risk sports. An injury-prone hero sees his or her injury as a sign of strength and endurance and takes a martyr's role by continuing to compete despite his injury and secures admiration with a ready-made excuse.

In addition, a child who hates sport but cannot tell his parents will use the threat of injury as a weapon, for example the young gymnast with 'backache' or the butterfly swimmer with painful shoulders may be seeking an 'out' from a sport that they no longer enjoy. Also, there are competitors who fear competitions so much that they need to be injured. When injured, they then avoid confrontation but can remain a member of the squad with their ego intact. In a team sport their mates can use the injury as an excuse for their failure.

Sometimes injuries are psychological. There is no real hurt, but the sufferer is unreliable and may present his 'injury' at any time. In addition, an injury can be used to avoid training, because the person wishes to cause problems for his coach or for his team, or because he wishes to avoid unfavourable comparison with others.

Occasionally one comes across the anxious coach whose over-concern for an athlete's well-being can, in turn, produce anxiety and tension in his athletes, who are then prone to injury.

Personality types have a lot to do with attitude to injury. Extroverts tend to be impulsive, optimistic with a high pain threshold and tend to ask 'When can I play again?' Whereas introverts tend to be apprehensive, have a low pain tolerance, overact and tend to ask 'Can I play again?' In addition, athletes are particularly vulnerable at a time when their overall athletic performance is in decline. After the age of 25 years, in many sports, we are in decline. Thank goodness in sailing there is usually a less demanding class to turn to!

Sod's syndrome

When all has been done that should have been done, then something will go wrong! In the case of sailors, a competitor will be injured by fooling about. This is most likely during the work up to an important event – probably when abroad when the sailor becomes bored with all-day training and tuning prior to racing. The coach should be vigilant at all times of the day and night. A variety of non-standard training routines and diversions must be devised to combat boredom. It is essential that physical training is maintained, though the time of day may have to change. Also, athletes in training regularly secrete substances (endorphins) within their circulation to which they become 'addicted' and which gives them a sense of euphoria or a 'high'. When they stop training, they miss these secretions and become moody and depressed. The time just before a competition is no time for a mood change.

Sailors should be aware, too, that progressive loss of muscle tone occurs rapidly especially after a long drive to a venue or when sleep is lost. The maintenance of a regular pattern of physical activity protects against mental stress. Prolonged periods in a car, plane, coach etc, in a slumped sitting posture require corrective back extension routines before taking to the water.

Diet and the dinghy racer

Linked very closely to your fitness training programme will be your nutrition. Yes, it does matter what you eat and drink during training and competition in order to get the best possible performance from your body at the right time. Therefore you should include consultation with a nutritionist during your fitness training. But by rule of thumb, four days before the first race you need to consider your nutritional programme – loading carbohydrates, ready to burn it all off during the event.

A key point to remember here: After burning off loads of energy you must top up your carbohydrates within 60 minutes otherwise you will lose your carbohydrate level dramatically and not recover them enough in readiness for the following day's racing. Liquid is also an important factor. You need to drink plenty, perhaps more than you think.

It helps to think of nutrition as six groups: *protein*, *fat* and *carbohydrate* (the bulk components) plus *minerals* (most of which are trace elements), *vitamins* and *water*. Stories circulate about the special benefits to be had from diets high in each one of these groups. Extra protein is said to build more muscle, extra fat is believed to keep you warm, 'carbohydrate loading' is claimed to give you endurance, others think the same about extra iron ... and extra vitamins, well they are claimed to enhance every physical prowess there is! Let us look at the bulk components in turn.

Protein

You certainly don't need to eat 10 eggs and 2kg of steak a day! The huge protein intakes of some athletes have little value except publicity. There is quite a lot of protein in wholemeal bread, vegetables (notably beans) and nuts; and, of course, there is a great deal in fish, yoghurt or cheese, and in milk. All of us like some of these foods, and many of us like all of them. So you can see that by eating a varied diet you should automatically eat enough protein, even if you are a vegetarian. Only if you are a vegan – a vegetarian who abstains even from dairy products and eggs – will you need to take extra care about getting sufficient protein. Probably the only other group today who may risk deficiency in the developed world are extremely faddy children but even here, a little extra of one protein source, milk for example, will compensate for the absence of others, such as meat and eggs.

Protein is not primarily a fuel, so it is not normally used to provide energy. It is only needed to build or repair tissue. No adult who can afford a sport like sailing is likely to eat insufficient protein.

Fat

Eating extra fat is not the best way to keep yourself warm. If you have really become skinny, you can put on a bit of insulation (and build your energy reserve) just as effectively by eating carbohydrates, with less risk to your arteries in later life. The body is able to turn extra carbohydrate into fat, though it cannot turn extra fat into carbohydrate.

You certainly need some fat – partly for its own contribution to nutrition and partly for the vitamins it carries (see below). However, as with protein, it is hard *not* to take in all the fat you need. Not only do we spread it on bread and use it in baking, it is present in meat, eggs and whole milk, as well as in nuts and chocolate and, of course, we fry things in it.

Carbohydrate

This is the main fuel food, so eat lots of it! Bread, cakes, all forms of cereals, fruit, beans and root vegetables, sugars, syrups and sweets – these are the principal carbohydrate foods. All give you energy, and none will make you fat as long as your energy output matches your intake. Stock up in advance; the meal before a big race should be particularly rich in carbohydrate. In addition if the race will be long, or there are to be two, back-to-back, take more carbohydrate-rich food with you in the boat.

A word of warning, however: there are two categories of carbohydrate – complex and simple. The simple carbohydrates are syrup and sugar, of which the simplest of all is glucose. The simpler the carbohydrate, the more rapidly it is absorbed by the body and the more rapidly it can be used. Take glucose in *small* doses (single tablets) every 20 minutes, or eat complex carbohydrates such as fruit, raw carrots, or filled baked potatoes or rolls.

Carbohydrate loading

This technique, also called glycogen loading, was developed by Saltin in Sweden in the 1960s. It is well established for long-distance cyclists, swimmers and skiers, and is practised by many marathon runners. Now some sailors are trying it too. The full 'Saltin Diet' consists of training strenuously during the first half of the week before a big race, while eating a low-carbohydrate diet. This exhausts the working muscles of their stocks of glycogen – the form in which they store carbohydrate. Then the athlete eats a high-carbohydrate diet on the last three days before the race while performing light training. The ultra-hungry muscles grab all the carbohydrate they can during this time. By race day they may have twice the glycogen content they would have had if the usual ratio of eating to training had been maintained throughout that time. The consequence is that during the race the muscles not only work longer, but they do not compete so much with the brain for blood-borne sugar (glucose), so many athletes feel that their minds stay sharper too. The brain's only source of energy is the blood sugar. If this falls, then the brain is less effective in decision making.

The Full Glycogen Boost/Saltin diet is designed for endurance runners not sailors! However, there is an easier modified Glycogen Boost diet which is quite suitable for sailors. This is to train as usual but to concentrate on a high carbohydrate intake in the three days before the regatta. In so doing, the exercise time to exhaustion will be significantly extended.

Do not forget that during exercise, the stores of glycogen are depleted in the exercising muscles, not in the ones that are having an easy time. Any new intake of glycogen is first deposited in the muscles that have been exercising, and is not shared out equally to every muscle in the body.

There will be some slight weight gain, as a result of carbohydrate loading, for either the full or the modified diet. Glycogen is stored with water in the body and is released following the demands of the exercise to fuel muscle work. In an endurance event this assists in combating dehydration, and it is possible that, in a marathon, the boost diet will benefit the body by preserving body fluid levels.

If, on the first day of a regatta the winds are light your glycogen stores will not be significantly depleted. However, if the winds are strong, you may score over those who arrived late at the event either having eaten little food, or lots of the wrong type in the preceding two days. The important point is that you start each day of racing with a high level of stored glycogen. If your energy stores become depleted you will still be better off than the competitor who starts with their stores low.

Body management

'Body management' has become an important part of many sports. We learn to 'manage' the dinghy by making adjustments to suit the prevailing conditions. We 'manage' the race strategy. We 'manage' the post-race protest situation. We 'manage' the getting to and from the venue and we 'manage' the repairs required in the event of gear failure. Yet few give thought to assisting the body to manage. For some reason we expect it to do the job itself. In fact we often go out of our way to make the task more difficult by arriving tired, late and hungry at an important event.

Let us look at a few basic facts relating to diet and sport.

- Work requires energy which is derived from body stores. The first available source of energy is chemical and will not last the whole of a 100 metre race. Glycogen, stored in the muscles and liver, provides the next source of energy. The human energy balance is shown by:

> Body energy intake =
> Body energy expended
> *plus or minus*
> Energy stored

  In other words, we may eat too little, too much or just enough for a particular task. Of the body's total energy intake, 60 per cent is needed to 'run the body' while 10 per cent is used for digestion.
- Extra carbohydrate, either complex or simple, eaten during the three days before a major event, may improve endurance capacity by up to 25 per cent.
- Ideally, carbohydrate is taken as wholemeal bread, muesli, cereals, pasta, brown rice, fresh or dried fruit and vegetables, beans, peas, lentils and potatoes. These are unrefined complex carbohydrates. Cakes, biscuits and sweets should not provide the bulk of carbohydrate intake but are convenient and pleasant as booster snacks.

- When glycogen is burned in a working muscle, lactic acid (LA) is formed. Accumulating LA limits muscular work and LA is formed much earlier in an untrained than a trained person.
- The heart rate is lower on a high-carbohydrate diet. Adrenaline levels are lower on a high-carbohydrate diet.
- Most people eat too much fat. One-third of our food intake is generally in the form of snacks and, although you may not realise it, one-third of those snacks will be fat. If you are trying to reduce weight, reduce your fat intake, but you may have to increase your carbohydrate intake considerably to allow you to sustain training. When eating meat, choose lean cuts, or leave the fat.
- Alcohol significantly reduces the liver's capacity to re-synthesise glycogen.

A Sports Nutrition Symposium at Lausanne in 1991 noted the composition of diets (below).

	UK households Actual (1989)	COMA Recommended (1984)	LAUSANNE Sports people (1991)
Carbohydrate	45%	50%	60–70%
Fat	42%	35%	20–25%
Protein	13%	15%	10–15%

An endurance athlete in training requires 10 grams carbohydrate per kilogram body weight per day and up to 1.5 grams protein per kilogram plus some fat. Few sailors will require these quantities. But if you are very active at work and do other sports as well as sailing, you may find that you will get tired unless you raise your carbohydrate intake.

A tired athlete cannot train. The body is too busy coping with its problems to spare the energy required for 'adaptation', which is what your training is all about.

Anorexia

There exists a condition known as post-exercise anorexia, or loss of a wish to eat, which prevents the early intake of further carbohydrate after a sports event. This is important especially to sailors who are competing in a series because they lose the opportunity to immediately 'top up' their glycogen levels. There is a phase of accelerated replenishment in the first hours after exercise which then falls significantly. So if you eat nothing for several hours after your race, it is impossible to get your stores back to normal in 24 hours. The eventual outcome is that towards the end of a week of heavy weather sailing you are going onto the water with energy stores maybe only two-thirds of what they were on the first day of racing. Bearing in mind that you have trained hard for the event and are in top physical condition, having spent many hours in general fitness and on the hiking bench, it seems a pity that you throw the series for want of better 'body management'!

Refuelling

Feeding after the event must start at once. If the course is a long way from the shore you must take food with you rather than lose the early hours of rapid glycogen replacement.

This is illustrated in the diagram (right) taken from the excellent publication *Nutrition for Sport* by Steve Wooton (Simon & Schuster).

Vitamin requirements of the athlete, sailor or otherwise, are adequately provided by the average diet. Scientific papers abound which, from time to time, advise extra of one or another vitamin but in most circumstances enough is enough. Remember that some vitamins are dissolved in fat and some in water. Those in water may be stored in the body less efficiently, as is the case with vitamin C. However, the sailors that this book is written for are unlikely to suffer from scurvy as in Nelson's day!

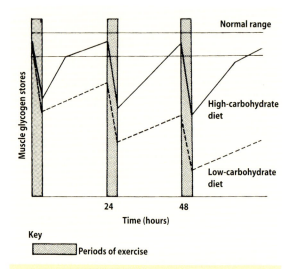

The effect of different amounts of carbohydrate in the diet on the refuelling of muscle glycogen following three bouts of exercise within a 72-hour period. There is a significant difference between the rate of refuelling on a high-carbohydrate diet and one that is insufficient in carbohydrate.

Mineral requirements are also provided in the average diet, though in young female (sailing) athletes there may be a requirement for extra iron and calcium. Remember that there is some extra value in the type of iron found in lean beef, fish and chicken meats. This is 'haem iron', which is a little different to the mineral iron found in iron tablets. While there is adequate calcium found in a pint of milk per day this is, of course, fatty. Female athletes are advised to drink a pint of skimmed milk daily which will provide the calcium without adding extra fat to their diet. It is not advised that sailing or indeed any other athletes should take daily iron tablets without their doctor's approval.

It is often stated that in the UK sailing climate, extra salt is unnecessary because it is often cold and so there will be less likelihood of undue sweating and consequent fluid/salt loss. We have, however, progressed from wearing shirts and shorts to remarkable thermally-efficient sailing clothing. The micro-climate between the skin and the wet suit, dry suit or thermal longjohns etc is the climate that matters. Thus on a cold day we can still suffer from heat exhaustion if sailing hard in a strong wind and unable to ventilate the protective layers. We can lose much body fluid and some electrolytes, so you should drink one of the many isotonic drinks that are on the market. If that evening you feel the urge for a little extra salt on the tuna salad, it is probably because you need it.

Fluid levels are critical for performance in all active sports. Of our body weight, 70 per cent is composed of water; 50 per cent of this is in the tissue cells, 15 per cent in the spaces between the cells and 5 per cent in the blood. The fluid compartments are interchangeable. They can allow for six pints of beer in, or six pints of sweat out. We can sweat three pints per hour. If we sweat a lot and do not replace the fluid, dehydration leads to an increased heart rate, making us begin to feel distressed sooner. This water loss is also associated with a rise in body temperature of nearly 1°C. We then begin to suffer distress from overheating.

Dehydration is not good for a top-class competitor. Look at the colour of your pee – if it is dark yellow, you are close to being, if not already, dehydrated. So get those fluids down you. However, it is very important to drink smaller amounts frequently, rather than lots all at once. Avoid alcohol and caffeine as these are diuretics. Non-caffeine energy drinks are the best as they give you something in return – water just keeps you alive! Do not allow yourself to become dehydrated as you will lose both concentration and performance ability.

Sailing championship competitors are advised to weigh themselves night and morning. A loss of one kilogram of weight is equal to one litre of fluid. This has to be replaced. Remember that thirst is a late symptom of dehydration. By the time you feel thirsty you are already dehydrated, your pulse is rising and your body is ill-equipped to handle the stress of competition. The sailor-athlete requires one litre of water a day to efficiently run the body. Plus an extra litre for every hour of training or competition. Sailors may not be endurance athletes but in their protective clothing they are susceptible to considerable fluid loss especially on a hot day. The answer is to drink as much water as you can to counter dehydration.

Fortunately, both our carbohydrate and our water requirements can be solved by the use of glucose polymer drinks. These contain long chain molecules of carbohydrate that do not taste sweet like sugar – an important factor when you are feeling thirsty. The carbohydrate and water are absorbed by the stomach and rapidly distributed round the body. The drink should be made up in weaker dilutions in hot weather, but stronger in cold weather when extra energy is needed. A 250 gram container of dry glucose polymer powder such as Caloreen (Roussel) would make many drinks and is far less expensive than the ready-made flavoured sports drinks.

Strengths of carbo drinks in relation to climate

Atmospheric temperature	% of carbo in drinks
Hot/warm 28°C	2%
Humid 25°C	4%
Warm 20°C	8–10%
Moderate/cold 20°C	12–14%

- In warm humid conditions, drinks should contain less carbo powder.

- In cold weather training, the concentration of powder may be increased to provide more energy.

- You should experiment to see what dilution suits you best in certain conditions.

- Plain water will not be absorbed as quickly as the carbo drinks. If you mainly need fluid replacement, use 5% powder to water.

Weight reduction

If you are trying to reduce weight, do not do this before a major event as it may affect your mood. Research has shown that when trying to train and compete while losing weight, the athlete may become more depressed, angry and tired. If you are training and working physically hard, as well as sailing, and you find that your weight is falling and you are tired, it is probably because your carbohydrate intake is too low. Increase it and see if your weight stabilises and your vigour returns. If it doesn't you may be over-training. Take a complete rest from training and sailing for a week before you begin again with a modified programme.

Recovery from exercise

As we already know, muscle glycogen is restored after 24 hours of recovery only if you start soon enough. Liquid and solid carbohydrates are equally effective over the first five hours of recovery. If you don't feel hungry after a race, take the carbohydrate as glucose polymer liquid – one gram of polymer per kilogram of body weight immediately after exercise. Then repeat every two hours for up to six hours. Use simple sugars (sweets, cakes or biscuits) to supplement carbohydrate intake if you don't feel like eating a bulky, unrefined carbohydrate meal.

Don't sail for an hour back to shore, fill in a protest form, chat with friends, go for random sail measurement etc and then have your first food, several hours after the race has ended. If you do, you are already a loser in the energy stakes for the race next day.

Additional issues

Drug abuse: This is an area of great concern to both competitors and coaches and one that is often overlooked. But do so at your peril! Drugs in sport are like an area of quicksand – always on the move. Even the doctors involved with athletes find it difficult to keep up with the changes. Caution is the key word here. Before you *ever* take any drug for whatever reason, even when supplied by your own GP or hospital, check with your coach/team doctor that it is not included on the latest list of banned substances. Always ensure that you have a copy of the most recent ISAF/WADA banned list with you (this varies from year to year and can normally be acquired from the National Authority). Even address the issue of too many cups of coffee which could give you a positive result!

Also, do not forget that if you are under medication when you go to an event, it must be declared with a signed letter from the Royal Yachting Association honorary medical officer and must be handed in to the organising authority prior to the start of the event. It is amazing, in recent times, how often top athletes in yachting have forgotten to do this and have been panicking to get a letter of authority sent out to them halfway round the world at the last minute! Other information on drugs can be obtained by visiting the ISAF website (www.sailing.org).

Medical/dental checks must be kept up to date. The last thing you need is to suffer from either a medical problem or toothache at a major event, so keep on top of this by having regular check-ups.

Body weight can be an issue for major events. This needs to be monitored at all times. You should know what weight you should be and keep yourself within that framework. I hate seeing sailors running around the local principality in dry suits on the morning of the first race – absolutely not the way to lose a few kilos. Body temperature is also often an issue at major events. How many times I have come across competitors who are either too hot or too cold to perform? I have lost count over the years. You must always make sure that your body temperature is right so that you can perform to the best of your ability. Being either too hot or too cold is not good enough; make sure that you have got the correct kit for the conditions of the day.

Relaxation: This is a very important part of your self-preparation programme. What do you do to relax when at events? We all have our own personal strategies, so make sure that yours are in place when you are at the venue. The worst case scenario is when you are held out on the water by the race committee, waiting for the wind to settle down. Think about how you will pass the time away while waiting and yet still be mentally alert and ready to win the race when the postponement flag comes down two hours later! The same is just as relevant when you are ashore. Work out the best way for you to relax and be prepared to take time out to do it.

Food is obviously a very important part of your well-being and not to be overlooked. When travelling to events abroad, you need to be very careful about what you eat and drink. There have been too many occasions in the past where endless hours of training, and vast amounts of money, have been wasted when a competitor has not been able to take part because of food poisoning or some other complaint. This is always very disappointing. So be warned: our stomachs are sometimes not accustomed to foreign foods and drinks and this is one item that both competitors and coaches must consider in the 'what if' scenario! Is there the possibility of taking your own food and liquid supplies with you to avoid any problems?

Sleep is a major issue when at events and many competitors suffer here, especially when having to sleep in a strange bed. It may take three to four days to acclimatise yourself before you will get a good night's sleep, so try to arrive at the venue in good time before Race 1 in order to overcome this problem. The number of hours' sleep that one requires is very much a personal issue. I have known people to have as little as four hours and then go out and win a race, whereas others have needed at least eight hours before they can do the same. Whatever the amount of sleep you need, make sure that you get it, because if you are losing sleep, then you are not going to perform at your best. So make sure that your accommodation is of a good enough standard and not above a disco that closes at 5am!

Daily routines play a major part in your success at events. It is always good to get into that routine as soon as possible after arrival at the event and after you have recovered from the travelling. If flying long distances, to New Zealand for example, allow at least a clear four days to get over the body clock issues (jet lag) before settling into your daily routine. A good booklet on this subject, *The Travelling Athlete*, has been produced by the British Olympic Medical Centre (www.olympics.org.uk). Part of your daily routine should include you being the first boat on the water and the first boat off. All part of the psychological warfare against your opponents! Having prepared ourselves physically for the most challenging sport in the world, we must now prepare ourselves mentally.

Psychology

Being mentally tough plays a major role in being successful and the higher up the ladder you climb, the tougher it becomes! Sports psychology has in the past helped many athletes to overcome certain barriers, as it will in the future. If an athlete has any issues that a sports psychologist can help with, then they should contact those working with their National Authority. Most common issues may just be those of goal setting, relaxation, motivation, determination or controlled aggression. These are various issues where the psychologist can help and, once again, these can be built into your training programme if required. Not everyone needs this support so only consult a psychologist if you feel that it would benefit your campaign. Otherwise, focus on all the other aspects of preparation in the time frame that you have available to you.

Attitude: You must have a positive attitude at all times. Positive thinking brings positive results, negative thinking will bring you negative results. Surround yourself in a positive atmosphere; place yourself within a positive circle not allowing anything negative to enter.

Determination: Having the determination to do well and see the task in hand carried out to the best of your ability at all times will play a major role in your campaign.

Controlled aggression: An internal part of your makeup, you need to have controlled aggression to be in the right place at the right time, whether it is on the starting line or elsewhere on the race track.

Motivation: Getting that gold medal is enough to motivate any top competitor. If you want it, go and get it. The world is your oyster! If you don't want it, adjust your training programme accordingly, along with your budget.

Commitment: You must be totally committed to the end of the programme otherwise why bother wasting all that time, effort and money for nothing? So before

When preparing for a gybe set, make sure that the spinnaker is being hoisted as soon as you start to bear away. Be ready to human guy it to fill it while the pole is topped and the genoa is dropped.

INSET: Windsurfing is a discipline where in 20 knots of wind, and two races a day, ONLY THE FITTEST WILL WIN!

setting out on this mission, make sure that you have the commitment to see it through to the end – win or lose. One thing that annoys most sailors is the person who says that he will commit, then legs it halfway through the programme – not good for your CV!

Concentration: Required by both helm and crew. Helms will need to have narrow external concentration whereas the crew will need broad external concentration. Both helms and crew will also have broad internal concentration.

Confidence: You must have the confidence to do well which you will have, after you've completed your training programme. Be confident that you can win, but never go to an event *expecting* to win or do well. If you do you will fail, as you will be overconfident and start making mistakes. Your mind must be like an open parachute, both on and off the water. Confidence breeds confidence. Only the fittest, both physically and mentally, will win! Believe that you *can* do well and that you *are* good enough to win.

Anxiety levels: At events these can be high, especially with younger racers, but they will subside as you gain more experience. If you do suffer, just heave to in the starting area, stand up and do some deep breathing exercises. At the same time, visualise the race you are about to begin and remember all the races in the past which you have won or done well in.

Evaluate: Everything! Keep on revisiting strengths and weaknesses, maintaining strengths and improving your weaknesses. Evaluation of your training programme should always be in the forefront of your mind.

Visualisation: Visualise how you are going to sail the race before you start. Then when you are on the race track, it might actually happen as it should, to the best of your ability.

Focus on your own job and not on others'. If you begin to lose focus because you are getting tired or dehydrated, have something in place between your port and starboard earlobes to help you refocus immediately! Loss of focus or concentration is the beginning of a poor performance.

Communication: When racing in ships with more than one sailor aboard, it is important to keep communication at a low level. The less talking there is on a ship, the better the performance. This applies even more so on the larger vessels with, let's say, 10 racers aboard. As the crew size grows in number, there should be well-organised communication. As an example: the bow man, the mast man, the tactician, plus a voice off the rail calling the pressure/waves and, downwind, the spinnaker trimmer talking to the helm. The helmsman's job is to sail the ship as fast as possible in a straight line as directed by the tactician. Therefore he/she does not have to say a thing all the way round the track!

Visualise what you are going to do before you start to do it. Focus on your own job and not someone else's.

Expectations: Too high? At the end of a day's training/racing it is always important to finish on a high, never on a low, in order to be mentally ready for the following day. There will be days when things do not go to plan, which is the same for everyone. Never forget – stay in a POSITIVE frame of mind!

Leadership: Your commitment and determination must come through and be seen to do so. Establish goals and roles; communicate these to the rest of the ship and agree how you are going to achieve them.

Roles: Understand your responsibilities and what you need to achieve in the role you have been given. List the areas in which you are involved and then break down these areas and go over them in your head until you are certain you know, in minute detail, each manoeuvre.

'What if' scenarios: You can think of numerous, so be ready with the answers! What if the prop shaft drops out of the car while on the French motorway and the car is British-made?! What if the main halyard breaks while on the way out to the start?! What if the ship, or part of it, does not make it through the measurement tent?! What if you tear the spinnaker during the first race of a three-race day, where will the spare one be?! What if you have a bad day on the race track – how are you going to pick yourselves up ready for the next day's racing?! etc. Make up your own, 'what if' emergency list – it will come in handy one day. If things do happen you will be prepared because you have already thought about the answers – all part of a winning campaign.

Psychological warfare: There can be plenty of this flying around an event, easily created either by the media or between competitors. As a competitor, I rarely read the yachting press because it often related a total misinterpretation of what was actually said or meant at the time.

One classic story of psychology between competitors involved a British and a European racer. The European was fed up with arriving at the boat park each morning only to see the Brit on his way in from training, so he decided that he would get up early the next day and be out training first. However, the British competitor heard about this and got up really early the following morning and, sure enough, the European arrived down at the boat park early next morning, only to see his British rival coming in with navigation lights on! The British competitor won the gold medal, having blown away the European psychologically! You can win events ashore before they even start!

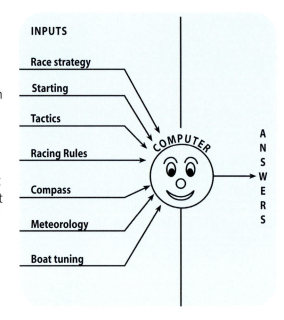

To sum up, pace yourself in both your training and eventing programme. You do not want to reach the brick wall just before your major event and be burned out! Burn out can easily be achieved by the following:

• Too much sailing.
• Too much training.
• Emotional stress.
• Illness.

If you do reach this point, then it is time to take a break, go and do something else with your life until the will to race returns. Then come back and start where you left off. You will never forget how to sail. All it will need is a little polishing up, and getting back to your training programme! Above all, never forget to *enjoy* your sailing first, think about your performance second, and identify your strengths and weaknesses. Work on the weaknesses while maintaining your strengths, train regularly and focus on specifics. Concentrate on learning *how* to win, not *what* to win.

FAIL TO PREPARE – PREPARE TO FAIL!

3
Boat Preparation

This is critical to your overall success in the sport, and is highly placed in our training programme in order to ensure the following:

- ❏ **Always** have a legal ship.
- ❏ **Never** suffer gear failure.
- ❏ **Always** be to the forefront with the latest technology.
- ❏ **Always** have the best possible hull.
- ❏ **Always** have the best spars.
- ❏ **Always** have the best sails.
- ❏ **Always** have the best foils.
- ❏ **Always** have the best fittings.

So, first you must establish who is going to build the boat? When do you want to take delivery (add at least one month to the date you have been promised!)? Who is going to produce the spars? Whose sails do you want? Again, allow extra time. Where, when and by whom will it be measured, if required, within the class rules?

Once you have acquired your ship, the majority of your spare time is going to be spent looking after her and keeping her in top racing condition. The larger and more complicated your vessel then, of course, the more hours you will need to spend working on her.

At the outset of a campaign, it is best to divide the ship into specific areas and make individuals responsible for looking after their own area. Then, when the ship goes to sea, they will know that she is ready for racing. I suggest to skippers that, before their ship leaves the dock, they go to the key personnel on board and ask each if their part of the ship is ready for racing. The answer should always be 'Yes' but if were to be 'No' you are in a 'What if' scenario and you should seriously consider their inclusion in the crew.

Hull: This must be fair and well polished or wet and dried (personal choice).

Spars: They must be the best for the job. Polished and as aerodynamic as possible. In the dinghy world, any terminals for trapeze wire or shrouds should be taped over so that they do not come out during a capsize.

Sails: Choose the best available for the conditions expected at the venue (flat or choppy water).

Fittings: As few as possible to reduce the risk of gear failure and to reduce the overall weight of the boat. All the fittings must be checked daily for fatigue or becoming loose. Ensure that you have sufficient spares with you as they can cost 'an arm and a leg' on some foreign shores!

Rigging: Both standing and running rigging must never let you down. Check, check and double-check after each day's racing especially when it has been blowing the dogs off their leads!

Measurement: Be confident that, when applicable, the ship will pass measurement on arrival at the event. The most common faults for those ships that have to go through measurement are:

• Being underweight.
• Foils which are either too thick or too thin.
• Spars with black bands missing.
• Sails with numbers in the wrong place.
• Buoyancy.

I wish I had a pound coin for every sail number or letter that I have had to move by two or three millimetres because the sailmaker has put them in the wrong place, or for every time I've moved the black band on a mast or boom! You do not need that type of aggravation at an event, so eliminate it from the programme.

There are numerous other pitfalls to look out for, especially where hull construction is concerned. When in hotter climates, do not leave your foils lying in the sun as they will swell. If, when measured, they are found to be too thick, put them in the nearest freezer for a couple of hours and then take them back and they should get through this time!

Another measurement nightmare is a sail being too large in certain areas. If you find that your spinnaker is too large, put it in an airing cupboard overnight and it should measure OK the following morning!

Measurement is an issue for many classes at major events, so please allow the time to get through it and make any necessary corrections. I cannot emphasise enough how important it is to be continually working on your ship so that you are always confident that you have the best possible racing machine and that she will never let you down – even if you have an event of 20 knots of wind all week.

Gear failure is not part of a champion's programme.

More words of wisdom (having learned from other people's mistakes): **Never turn up at the event with untried or untested new kit. It spells disaster!**
I remember one famous occasion when this happened, arriving at a championship with a brand new boat. As she went through measurement the measurer asked, 'Where is the buoyancy in the side tanks?' The builder had only forgotten to put it in! We solved the problem by filling the buoyancy tanks with inflated beach balls ... Highly irregular! If the measurer had said 'No' to this solution, we would have travelled a long way, spent a lot of money and achieved nothing!

Hull: outer finish, stiffness, weight

The outer hull must be fair and have a racing finish. It is no good arriving at a high-level championship event with a hull that is dirty, scratched and chipped, or with protruding screw heads or with slot gaskets and self bailers not faired in, and then wonder why boat speed is below par! The outer hull should be cleaned with fine abrasive polish to produce a slightly dulled matt finish to reduce the surface drag and allow for better water-to-hull separation.

Today's boat manufacturers are using more advanced materials and superior building techniques to produce stiffer boats that last much longer than previously. This is

When you get the chance, remember to tidy up all the string lying around so that you don't end up with a pile of spaghetti!

good news for competitors, but unfortunately such boats do not last for ever – especially if they are not looked after and transported carefully to and from events. It is important to take care of the hull and its stiffness. Check it frequently by turning it upside down or on its side and, using the ball of your hand, try pushing in the hull around the area of the mast, back to the after end of the centreboard case where it is going to take the pounding on the waves. If it has gone soft in this area, it is time to change as performance will have been lost. However, softness is not a problem in the stem and stern areas, where the boat is lighter.

The boat's weight is obviously fairly critical, especially in performance dinghies, and it is important to try to keep the boat down to near minimum weight. This is not normally a problem. It is advisable whenever possible, perhaps during the winter months, to air out your boat with the aid of a heater or a light bulb let into the side tanks or forward hatch. Do not arrive at an event with a boat that is underweight and that already has maximum allowed correctors fitted! If you do, you will definitely have a problem bringing it up to weight.

Spars

In strictly one-design classes, all spars are supplied by the one manufacturer and should therefore be identical. However, even here, all-up weights have been found to be different, resulting in lighter, softer, heavier or stiffer spars. So if you are a lightweight helm and/or crew, if possible try to acquire the lighter, softer, more bendy spar; and vice versa for heavier weights. In the development classes, the world's your oyster! What are *your* specific requirements? Ask yourself the following questions:

- How much will it cost?
- Which manufacturer?
- Which section?
- Stiff mast sideways and fore-and-aft?
- Soft mast sideways and fore-and-aft?
- What is your all-up bodyweight?
- Flat or choppy water venue?
- Flat or full mainsail?
- What is the class World Champion/National Champion using?

Once you have answered all these questions, you will be able to reach a decision. You may even decide on a mast for flat water venues and one for the open sea – if allowed in your class rules (and your budget!).

To help you select the most suitable mast, on the next three pages you will find information on various mast sections available from leading dinghy mast manufacturers, used internationally by many top competitors.

Super Spars mast selection

The correct choice of Super Spars for any particular class is determined by the bend characteristic you require, relative to the smallest section (for minimum windage), and minimum weight. You will need to take account of your sail shape and crew weight when making your spar selection and if there is any doubt seek advice. See table for size, weight and stiffness.

M1 is a flexible and light mast in the range. It is ideal for smaller dinghies and is very successful in National 12s, Cherubs, Gulls, Graduates, Solos, etc.

M2 is the real powerhouse combining lightweight and stiffness to produce a moderately stiff rig for most medium-size dinghies. This is already a very successful design for Javelins, Flying Fifteens, 505s and many other classes.

M3 has the same stiffness sideways as M2, but is more flexible fore-and-aft.

M4 is designed for classes requiring an all-round, stiffer-than-average spar, and is suitable for all boats needing a slightly stiffer spar than M2.

M5 is the ultimate, no-compromise Flying Dutchman spar.

M6 has swept the board in the International 14 fleet where it is proving to have just the right combination of strength, stiffness and light weight for this most demanding class. It is also ideally suited to large dinghies such as the Laser 16, small cruisers and even Micro Cuppers.

M7 is the new Super Spars section developed for the 1990s. Its low weight coupled with excellent sideways stiffness and medium fore-and-aft stiffness, produces a spar of outstanding performance potential, improving on the concept developed by the M3 to produce a spar with the optimum dynamic response required to match modern dinghy sails.

M8 has been developed as a more flexible Flying Dutchman mast.

M9 is the smallest lightweight section for use on Youth Trainer boats, eg the 405.

Super Spars mast dimensions			
Section	Size (mm)	Weight (kg/m)	Stiffness
M1	55 x 68	0.94	34
M2	57 x 72	1.05	44
M3	57 x 72	1.04	40
M4	57 x 72	1.15	47
M5	57 x 72	1.21	49
M6	61 x 74	1.19	55
M7	57 x 69	0.95	42
M8	55 x 69	1.14	44
M9	53 x 64	0.90	28

Super Spars boom dimensions		
Section	Size (mm)	Weight (kg/m)
B1	60 x 72	1.03
B2	60 x 82	1.08
B4	76 x 76	1.05
B5	69 x 95	1.50

Seldén aluminium section selection

Mast

	Section name	Section weight (kg/m)	Dimension fore/aft (mm)	Dimension athw (mm)	Stiffness fore/aft (cm⁴)	Stiffness athw (cm⁴)	Suitable for
	2420	0.78	61	50	10	7.5	Cadet, Feva, Snipe, Vaurien
	Electron	1	61	66	11	18	Splash, Flash
	Lambda	0.86	63	51	13	10	Vaurien, Teeny
	C	0.9	65	54	14	10	Lark, Solo, Firefly
	Kappa	0.91	67	55	16.5	12	420, Flying Junior
	E	1.17	70	54	19	14	Flying Dutchman, Wanderer, Wayfarer
	Cumulus	0.95	69	58	19.5	14	420, 470, 505, Albacore, Hornet, Fireball, Scorpion, Solo, RS200, RS400, GP14
	D Plus	1.03	73	57	19.5	14	Enterprise
	Epsilon	1.02	72	57	20	15.5	470, Osprey, Pirat
	Gamma	1.15	75	56	27	16	Flying Dutchman, Nomad

Boom

	Section name	Section weight (kg/m)	Dimension fore/aft (mm)	Dimension athw (mm)	Stiffness fore/aft (cm⁴)	Stiffness athw (cm⁴)	Suitable for
	2520	1.06	63	53	20	11	Solo, Vaurien, Firefly
	2628	1	72	63	26	16	420, Contender, Enterprise, Flying Junior, GP 14, Lark, Pirat, Snipe
	Olympus	1.02	72	66	29	17	420, 470, Scorpion, Comet Race
	2229	1.05	75	55	30	14	Contender, Europe, Snipe
	2633	1.06	85	66	40	18	505, Albacore, Fireball, Osprey, Flying Dutchman, Wayfarer, Snipe, Vaurien

Seldén carbon section selection

Mast

	Lower mast	Section weight (kg/m)	Fore/Aft dimension (mm)	Athw dimension (mm)	Fore/Aft equivalent I (cm⁴)	Athw equivalent I (cm⁴)	Suitable for
	Series 3	0.47–0.64	64*	52	18–27	15–23	Phantom, Merlin Rocket, Musto Skiff, 59er, Int. Canoe, Contender, FD
	CC079	0.80–0.91	79*	61	27–41	23–34	Int.14, K19
	Orbis	0.43–0.56	60*	60	16–24	15–23	OK, RS800, B14

*Dimension excluding track.

Boom

	Section name	Section weight (kg/m)	Dimension (mm)	Equivalent stiffness vertically (cm⁴)	Equivalent AWS (cm⁴)	Suitable for
	76	0.66	76	32	30	Phantom, Merlin Rocket, Musto Skiff, Int. Canoe.
	88	0.77	88	49	47	Int.14, K19, Contender

As the windward boat, 1740 must keep clear. 1715 cannot sail above her proper course if she established the overlap to leeward from clear astern.

Sails

Again, one-design classes have no choice; the sails are all supplied by the same manufacturer using the same weight of cloth and the only difference is how the sails are set up. For the development classes, there is yet another set of questions:

- Which sailmaker?
- What will the cost be?
- Flat water venue? If so, flatter sails/firmer leeches.
- Choppy water venue? If so, fuller sails/softer leeches.
- What mast? The mainsail luff curve needs to be matched to the bending characteristics of the mast to produce optimum shape and performance.
- What is the class World Champion/National Champion using?

When you have gathered all the necessary information, take it to your chosen sailmaker. You may well find that they are currently carrying out research and development in your particular class of boat. Ideally, try to use a sailmaker whose loft is situated close to you, so that you can develop a good relationship and visit the loft to discuss ideas and information. If possible, watch the sail being made – that way, you could learn a lot about your sails.

Foils

Here, technology has advanced enormously in terms of both design and materials. Keels, centreboards and rudders have, in recent years, been seen in various shapes and sizes. A variety of different materials are now being used, either throughout the foil or trailing or leading edges only, or a different material is used in the top section to that in the bottom section.

Once again, strictly one-design classes use a standard design and materials, whereas in the development classes there is much to be gained by having good foils. Look at what the top sailors are using; visit the top foil manufacturers and decide on the best shape and materials allowed in your class rules. When you have acquired your foils, make sure that they are finished off in the same way as your hull finish so that foils and hull become the same through the water.

Most sailors will, if their class rules allow, look for a maximum weight keel/centreboard and a minimum weight rudder blade in order to bring the boat up to weight and at the same time keep the centre of gravity of the boat as low as possible. However, it is important not to have the rudder blade so light that it snaps in the upper wind/sea state on a reach! Most under-canvased boats will go for a centreboard that is very stiff sideways for good pointing ability, whereas the overcanvased boats will prefer something softer in the mid to upper wind range, assisting the depowering of the boat and reducing weather helm, especially – if class rules permit – in the upper part of the board: stiff sideways, softer bottom sideways.

Centreboards and rudder blades are very expensive items and need to be looked after. When they are not in use, make sure that they are put in their bags or that, when left in the boat, the trailing edges of centreboards are protected. When visiting the hotter climates, do not leave them lying in the sun as they can easily twist, warp and even swell, and could therefore fail measurement. If this does happen, find a freezer to leave them in for an hour or so!

Fittings

There are numerous fittings to choose from, and which ones you finally acquire depends upon your personal budget. As a guideline, you should try to use as few as possible to reduce:

- Your overall budget.
- All-up weight of the boat.
- Risk of gear failure.

Wherever possible, make sure that all fittings are bolted on so that they cannot pull out. Also, make sure that after each day of use they are thoroughly washed in fresh water to get rid of any salt, sand, grit and dirt – especially all blocks and cleats. Maintenance of a boat will vary depending on how big the vessel is and how much equipment is on board. For example, maintaining an International 14 may take eight hours a week, whereas a Laser 1 may only take eight minutes!

Boat layouts can go from one extreme to the other in some classes: some with very few fittings, others a mass of rope, blocks and cleats. Try to keep your boat as simple as possible for the reasons already mentioned.

There are some ingenious systems to operate all the boat tuning controls in the development classes, and it is well worth spending some time at dinghy exhibitions, boat shows or in the dinghy parks at international events studying these systems to pick up good ideas – and even to better them.

Boat preparation is an on-going subject because ideas and fashion change with the developments in technology, materials and designs. You must always keep abreast of these developments if you are to stay at the front of the fleet.

In summing up this particular subject, be meticulous with your boat preparation. This variable alone has been responsible for many a failed campaign.

4
Boat Handling

Once you have prepared both yourself and the ship for the event, you need to be able to sail her across all the wind and the sea states. Whether it is flat water and 2 knots or big waves and 30 knots, you have got to be able to handle the ship in all conditions. If you sail an Optimist or an America's Cup boat, or anything in between, and you want to be the gold medallist at whatever level of competition, it is all about the mechanics of sailing the boat whether in a straight line or turning corners. You must know what you have to do and visualise it so that when you actually do it, it might happen as it should, to the best of your ability. Put the effort in and get the reward out.

Generally speaking, the British are normally good at boat handling. Why? Because we spend a great deal of time practising this during our training programme across both sea and wind range. I recall a top yachtsman asking, 'When will I be good enough to win a medal in my 470?' The answer: 'Come and see me when you have completed your 2000 hours' apprenticeship!' **Mileage, mileage and more mileage** is what it takes to make it to the top in any International class of racing machine. It is all part of the training programme and yet another variable to overcome.

Boat handling issues are:

❑ **Boat balance** – athwartships.
❑ **Boat trim** – fore and aft.
❑ **Sail trim**.
❑ **Tacking**.
❑ **Gybing**.
❑ **Spinnaker** – hoist, gybe, drop.
❑ **Mark roundings**.

Boat balance

In both dinghies and yachts, whether to balance the boat upright, slightly heeled to leeward, or slightly heeled to windward depends on the underwater shape of the hull and the wind speed and the sea state for each point of sailing ie beating, reaching and running. If your boat balance is wrong for the conditions of the day and the point of sailing that you are on, then your straight line boat speed will suffer.

Beating: Normally you should try to keep the boat as upright as possible while beating to windward for maximum power out of the rig. This will give you the best boat speed and pointing ability in the middle wind range.

In light airs it will generally pay to heel the boat slightly to leeward so that the sails take up their natural shape with the least amount of wind. This also reduces the wetted area of the hull in contact with the water, which will assist in increasing your hull speed through the water. The amount of heel in light airs depends very much on the amount of rocker there is built into the underwater design shape of the hull. In some classes, such as the Merlin Rocket or National 12, if you heel the boat too much you in fact increase the wetted area of the hull and therefore decrease your straight line hull speed.

Good boat balance to leeward in these light airs – try to reduce the windage by either getting team members down below or lying down. The helmsman could sit down to reduce the windage too – every bit helps.

At the start looking for maximum hull speed, crews should try their best to keep out of the slot area by getting as low down as possible.

In the upper wind range, you should now be doing everything possible to keep the boat as upright as you can, and extra hiking out is required in both dinghies and yachts. In order to keep the ship as upright as possible in the upper wind range, you must depower the rig, as required, so that you are not heeling too much with the boat sliding sideways over the water carrying too much weather helm. We will look at how best to do this under the variable of boat tuning in Chapter 5. One thing worth noting while beating to windward in light winds is that, in some ships when there is enough wind to fill the sails (say 6 to 8 knots), it actually pays to heel the boat slightly to windward to get the rig directly above the centreboard/keel and sailing with a slight feel for lee helm. My mate Laurie Smith used to do it with good effect in the 470 class back in the 1970s. Try it within your training programme to see if it works for you.

Reaching in light airs: Again, balance the boat slightly to leeward, primarily to assist the sails to fill, and also, once again, to reduce the wetted area of the hull.

Running in light airs: This varies from class to class for all the right reasons. Generally, in the majority of classes, the boat needs to be balanced to windward to achieve the following:

That's better!

- To reduce the wetted area.
- To raise the outboard end of the boom higher off the water, thereby offering more sail area higher to catch the wind.
- To take the centre of effort of the rig more directly above the centre of lateral resistance of the boat.
- In the spinnaker boats, to allow the spinnaker to come from behind the mainsail and fill more easily.

If the wind is so light that the mainsail will not fill while balancing the boat over to windward, then heel it to leeward. Those who have spinnakers take them down and sail a slightly hotter angle to put more apparent wind across the sails. This will get you to the leeward mark quicker.

Medium winds to windward: In the medium wind, you are looking for maximum power and to achieve this you must balance the boat dead upright keeping her as flat as possible all the time.

Reaching in medium winds: Here, too, on this point of sailing you are looking for maximum power and trying to keep the boat dead upright to achieve this.

Running in medium winds: As with reaching for maximum power and drive, you should try to keep the boat dead upright, or slightly balanced to windward.

Beating in the upper wind range: While beating in the upper wind range, you will not be able to keep the boat dead upright, but you must try your best to do so. To achieve this, you will have to depower the rig as much as possible (see Chapter 5).

Reaching in the upper wind range: Boat balance dead upright, again not easy in the upper wind range, but you must do everything possible to achieve it. In the keelboats depower as much as possible by easing the kicker. If you still can't hold her relatively upright, reduce the amount of canvas. In the dinghies, ease the kicker. If still overpowered, raise the centreboard more to reduce the heeling moment of the boat.

Running in the upper wind range: Exciting times! The aim is to keep the boat as dead upright as possible. There are various factors that enable you to achieve this. The key ones are:

- Boat trim – maximum aft.
- Kicker – tight.
- Spinnakers – strapped down both tack and clew.
- Do not allow the spinnaker clew to go near the fore stay.
- Steer the boat under the rig.
- Dinghies – centreboard, not too high or low.

If you remember all these key points all the time, you might stand a chance of survival!

Boat trim

The fore and aft trim of the boat is critical for boat speed on each point of sailing, across both sea and wind range. It can be as effective in the light to medium-weight keelboats as it can be in dinghies. How much fore and aft depends very much on the design of the hull shape. For example, trim an Optimist too much by the bow and you start pushing too much water and slow down. Sit too far back in an Etchell on the running leg, in light winds, and the long overhanging transom creates too much drag and slows the boat down. You must appreciate the underwater characteristics of the boat when applying the correct amount of trim fore and aft for each point of sailing.

Beating in light winds – flat water: Trim the boat down by the bow to lift the after sections of the boat, ie the transom, off the water and reduce the amount of drag. The boat will be faster to windward.

Boat trim – maximum waterline length is good for boat speed on flat water.

Waves/confused sea: Trim the boat for maximum waterline length for maximum boat speed.

Beating in medium winds: Maximum waterline length on relatively flat water/short chop. In larger waves, trim slightly further aft to allow the bow to lift slightly and find its own way through the waves using less rudder to steer the boat. This is very effective in dinghies and light displacement yachts.

Good boat trim here is indicated by the clean exit of water away from the transom.

Beating in the upper wind range: Once again, maximum waterline length especially on flatter water/short chop venues. In bigger seas/waves, trim the boat slightly further aft as in the medium wind range. With maximum waterline length, the heavier displacement yachts like Dragons, and others of a long narrow shape, will find their own way through the waves with little assistance from the rudder.

Reaching in light winds: In flat water, trim down by the bow to lift the after section and transom off the water. Be careful not to over-trim by the bow, especially in boats with fatter/wider sections forward of the mast and those with rounded flat sterns above the waterline, as now you will begin to push too much water and go slower. Again, maximum waterline is needed in choppy/sloppy seas to maintain boat speed.

Reaching in medium winds: Maximum waterline length is needed on flat/short chop venues and in bigger waves/confused sea state. Trim the boat slightly further aft to help the bow lift over the waves.

Reaching in the upper wind range: Trim the boat further aft across the sea state range to lift the lee bow off the water. This allows you to bear away more easily using less rudder to turn the boat away from the wind when you are hit by a gust.

Running in light winds: In flat water, trim the boat down by the bow to reduce the wetted area and surface drag. This also works well in the bigger/heavier displacement yachts. Send heavier crew below and forward! Maximum waterline length is needed in sloppy/confused sea state.

Total concentration by both racers on sail trim, boat balance and boat trim. Impressive!

Running in medium winds: In flat water/short chop, you need maximum waterline length. In choppy seas, trim slightly by the stern.

Running in the upper wind range: Trim the boat down by the stern and focus on keeping the bow as high out of the water as possible to prevent the bow from becoming a rudder. As the boat rolls slightly, both the windward and leeward bows take on a lot of pressure forcing the bow off in that direction which requires the opposite force on the rudder to correct it. This combination of bow and rudder opposing each other slows down the boat and increases the rolling motion – very exciting! This combination alone can be responsible for the following broach or Chinese gybe – not good if you want a podium position!

Sail trim

This is critical for each point of sailing, whether you have one, two, three or more sails. You must always be ready to trim your sails in order to maintain maximum boat speed. Many times I have heard the same old story, 'We were going great up the first beat, but slower up the second'. No wonder when either the wind speed or sea state had changed – or both – but on board, in respect of the sail shape, nothing had changed. **Sails must be trimmed all the time to the course that is being sailed**.

Good boat balance, trim and slot shapes here with both the jib and the gennaker. The mainsail leech maybe a little too hard as shown by the top telltale stalling. If you want more speed, ease the kicker a little.

These are the basics of sail trim that are often forgotten while racing. Please, remember them:

To windward: **Jibs** are set up for the conditions at the time, halyard tension, barber haulers and lead block sheet tension. Once set up, the helmsperson steers to those settings, using the luff telltales to sail the boat as fast as possible. The windward telltales should always be streaming slightly above the horizontal and the leeward ones horizontal. Never use *green* telltales as you will always be on a header!

Mainsails on ships with more than one sail will be trimmed so that the upper telltale on the leech is streaming horizontally off the leech 80 per cent of the time and stalling 20 per cent. That is when the telltale disappears out of sight to leeward of the sail with the boom being kept on the centreline of the boat. Boats with high aspect ratio mains, where the distance between the mast and the leech of the main is only narrow, will not be able to achieve this. Here the top telltale will always be stalling; so try using the telltales lower down the leech, where the distance between the mast and leech is greater, so that it stands a chance of working.

Reaching: Both headsails and mainsails are now trimmed so that their leading edges are just thinking about lifting (that is with the wind on their leeward side). It is while on this point of sailing that the helm will be steering an erratic course when waves are present, as well as gusts of wind. Bear away in the gusts and/or with a wave and come up in the lulls and/or out of the trough of a wave. Now both the jib and main are being constantly trimmed for maximum boat speed. Total concentration is required here to gain distance on those who are not concentrating!

Ease the tack of the gennaker in the upper wind range to lift the bow out of the water.

Running: Headsails will be goosewinged (set opposite to the main). Mainsails will be maximised out and should be set at right angles to the masthead wind indicator.

Spinnakers/gennakers are thought by many to be the most exciting of all the sails and are fun to play with.

Reaching: Always kept eased to the curl. Spinnaker pole height is adjusted so that the two corners of the sail are the same height above the water.

Running: Always keep the pole at right angles to your masthead wind indicator. As the helm alters course using any existing waves, keep on easing the sail to the curl all the time striking it if she is about to collapse. In the upper wind range, never let the clew anywhere near the forestay, otherwise it could be swimming time with the capsize to windward! It is also critical while running in the upper wind range to keep both the tack and the clew of a spinnaker strapped down closer to the water, to lower the centre of effort of the sail. This, combined with over-trimming the sheet, will reduce the oscillation of the spinnaker from side to side and therefore, in turn, reduce the death roll! Gennakers, like spinnakers, will always be eased to the luff curl – the key thing here for the trimmer is calling the pressure in the sheet to the skipper. As the pressure increases, inform the helm so

Ease the clew outhaul on the main in the upper wind range to close the leech and reduce the rolling of the boat downwind.

that he can bear away and go with the gust. As it eases, call it, so that the helm can come up and maintain boat speed. The next key thing to address with the gennaker ships is how high or low to sail for the best VMG (velocity made good) downwind. Only mileage will give you the answer in your class of boat, for the conditions at the time. Basic guideline: the harder it is blowing, the deeper you go and vice versa when it goes lighter. When sailing against a foul tide, always try to sail deeper, even when in light winds, otherwise it will take forever to get to the leeward mark.

To learn more about how effective sail trim is to the hull, practise rudderless sailing by either tying the tiller amidships or taking it off. Rudderless sailing also teaches you more about the characteristics of the boat and just how important sail trim, along with boat trim and balance, is to turning the boat and thereby using less rudder and maintaining boat speed. Learning to sail your machine without a rudder may well do you a favour one day. I recall an occasion when young Andy Fitzgerald sailed his International 14 back from Bembridge to Chichester without a rudder and thanked us for showing him how to do it during his youth training because he made it home in time for his roast beef and yorkshire pudding!

Both crew roll the boat together keeping the mainsail in, easing the jib slightly using their body weight; now less rudder is needed to turn the boat.

Tacking

Tacking a boat across both the sea and wind range is an art, and there is much to be gained and lost here.

Roll tacking: Whether it is a lightweight dinghy or keel boat, roll tacking the boat properly will gain distance over the water over those who don't. We are talking several metres depending on how many tacks you might do throughout a race. The actual mechanics of tacking obviously vary depending on the type/size of boat and the number of people on board. However, the basic principles are the same whether you are in an Optimist or an IMX 40. The basics of a good roll tack are as follows: Use the hull shape and foils to their maximum efficiency to maintain hull speed throughout the

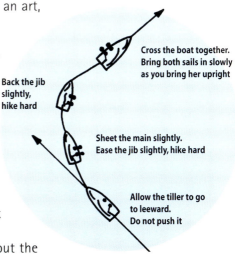

Cross the boat together. Bring both sails in slowly as you bring her upright

Back the jib slightly, hike hard

Sheet the main slightly. Ease the jib slightly, hike hard

Allow the tiller to go to leeward. Do not push it

tack. This means using body weight as well to assist the manoeuvre and the correct amount of rudder – not too much or too little. Use of the sails to assist the speed of the turn and boat balance and trim are crucial to a good roll tack.

Boat trim: Maximum waterline length.

Boat balance: From close-hauled to just before the eye of the wind, slight heel to leeward, allowing the lee bow to turn the boat towards the eye of the wind and therefore less use of the rudder is needed to maintain hull speed.

Sail trim: From close-hauled to the eye of the wind, ease the jib slightly. This gives you upper jib leech twist and helps to maintain hull speed. It also allows the bow of the boat to come towards the wind more easily; again, less rudder to turn the boat equals more hull speed into the tack.

Mainsails – from close-hauled to the eye of the wind, just sheet the main slightly harder. This helps to firm up the mainsail leech which pushes the stern of the boat to leeward and the bow to windward, again requiring less rudder to turn the boat into the tack and maintaining hull speed.

As you approach the eye of the wind. Boat balance to windward, in all dinghies and light displacement keelboats, with your best feature almost touching the water!

As you pass the eye of the wind. Allow the jib to back wind slightly while sitting on what was the windward side. This allows the bow to be brought swiftly down to the new close-hauled course. Crews, do not overdo this! If you do, you will slow the boat down as the helm has to correct the turn by using the rudder.

Boat balance: As the boat goes through the eye of the wind you will start to feel the ocean approaching the neck area! As it does, you are looking up at the rig thinking it is going to capsize on top of you. It is if you do not move now! Both helm and crew must immediately cross the boat together and pop out on the new windward side, bringing the boat back upright. While crossing the boat, the helm eases an armful of mainsheet and as he sits down on the new tack, pulls it back in to accelerate the boat out of the tack with both main and jib coming in together. Tacking on flat water is not an issue as you can go whenever it is clear to do so. However, in waves it is more critical that you get it right, otherwise you may well end up in irons or just stopping, having hit a wave badly.

The key points to remember are: Look at the waves approaching the weather bow. As the bow is lifted by a wave, the tiller should be on its way to leeward. With the wave now under the mast area, the bow must be going through the eye of the wind. As you bring the boat back upright out of the tack, you are now accelerating off the back of the wave that initially lifted the bow. When the sea state is confused, with waves all over the place, you must look for, and use, the larger ones.

Synchronised use of body weight moving together at the right time roll gybes the boat.

Gybing

Like roll tacking, this is yet another critical manoeuvre in the boat. If roll gybing is executed properly, distances can be gained or made over the opposition. To roll gybe efficiently, as you turn the boat away from the wind direction you must roll the boat over to windward not using too much rudder as this will slow down the boat. Let the weather bow of the boat do the turning for you.

The key points to remember, which obviously vary from class to class depending on the number of sails and bodies on the boat, follow.

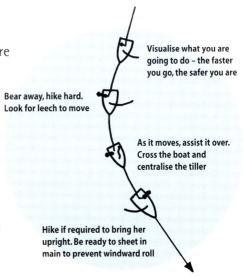

Visualise what you are going to do – the faster you go, the safer you are

Bear away, hike hard. Look for leech to move

As it moves, assist it over. Cross the boat and centralise the tiller

Hike if required to bring her upright. Be ready to sheet in main to prevent windward roll

Excellent use of body weight by both helm and crew to roll gybe the boat.

Singlehanders (centre mainsheet)

As you bear away, after first putting your foot across her, allow the boat to balance over to windward. Now look for the mainsail leech to want to move over to windward and, as it does, pull the mainsheet. As the boom comes across, be ready to move your best feature swiftly across the boat and park it on the new windward side, centralising the tiller as you cross, to prevent the boom end hitting the water as the mainsail fills on the new tack. Give the mainsheet a pull to maintain boat speed throughout. Before you ever execute this manoeuvre, make sure that the centreboard is in the correct position across both the wind and sea state range. The correct position being enough to stand on once you have capsized!

You can use the mainsheet in this way in both dinghies and small displacement keelboats but obviously not in larger ships as there will be too much pressure on the mainsheet, except in the light winds when it may be possible. Roll gybing is very effective in both the light and medium wind range. No need to bother in the upper wind range, in terms of boat speed throughout the gybe. In the upper wind range while gybing, all you need to remember is that the faster you are travelling as you go into the gybe, the safer you are and you stand an excellent chance of survival! If the

Coming out of the gybe, both crew bring the boat back upright together to maintain boat speed.

boat is going slow, as when you are between waves in a trough, you will not be able to gybe because the wind pressure on your sail plan will be at its maximum. If you do manage to gybe, you will be definitely be going for either a broach or a swim – or both!

Spinnaker hoists

Before even thinking about hoisting the spinnaker, please make sure that it has been packed and connected correctly! I wish that I had a fiver for every time I have seen it hoisted upside down. Even by the leader at a National Championship!

Prior to the hoist you want to try to sneak both the halyard and the guy out a little if possible to save time when the order comes to hoist. Aim to have the

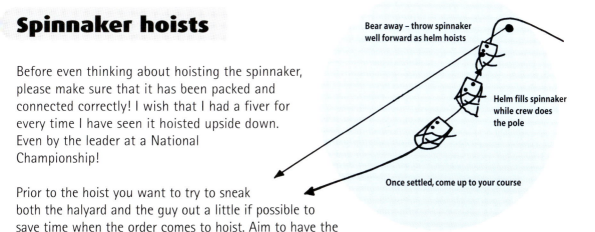

Bear away – throw spinnaker well forward as helm hoists

Helm fills spinnaker while crew does the pole

Once settled, come up to your course

spinnaker up and filled before exiting the 'two hull length circle' of the mark. In a perfect world, your final approach to the mark should be slightly above the lay line, so that you can pre-set the pole ready for the hoist. In some of the high performance dinghy classes this can even be done with the crew steering from the trapeze, while the helm goes forward to put up the pole. As soon as you bear away, the head of the spinnaker should be on its way up to the top. As it is being hoisted, the pole must be pulled back to get the spinnaker to fill. With the leeward hoist, do not over-ease the headsail as the spinnaker may well catch the foot, trying to drag the jib up with it, not good for those on the spinnaker halyard. For a gybe set, whether the spinnaker is to windward or to leeward, as you bear away and hoist, once it is up, the first thing that the crew must do is grab the guy and hold it out to windward so that the sail fills. Then he can grab the pole and put it on which will save the spinnaker from getting wrapped around both jib and forestay (very embarrassing!).

Running leg: As the ship starts to bear away the hoist commences as quickly as possible while at the same time the guy is brought back to get the air into the spinnaker and fill it. In the keelboats, when the spinnaker is approximately three-quarters up you can let go the genoa halyard which will fall onto the foredeck as it was not over-eased during the bear away – if it had been, it would cause too much friction while trying to hoist the spinnaker. Letting go the genoa halyard before the spinnaker reaches the top helps the spinnaker to fill quickly and reduces the risk of it getting twisted around the forestay. If the spinnaker fills before it is fully hoisted, just grind it all the way up on the winch, do not let it empty as this will lose that all-important boat speed and the gap which you have already created between yourself and the opposition.

Reaching leg: In keelboats, again sneak both the guy and the halyard, bear away for the hoist, guy sheeted to the end of the pole as the spinnaker is going up, as soon as it fills then come up to your proper course for the next mark.

Doublehanders (reach to reach gybe)

High approach, low exit is what is needed here to keep the spinnaker full throughout the gybing manoeuvre. If you cannot do this because of rules or tactical restrictions, then you must ensure that, during the turning circle, the spinnaker is rotated onto the new leeward side and does not go between the mast and the forestay! As you bear away, the crew must square the spinnaker pole back so that on completion of the gybe the spinnaker is completely on the new leeward side. When the gybe is completed, the helm takes both the guy and the sheet and fills the spinnaker while the crew transfers the pole. As soon as the pole is on, the crew takes the guy and cleats it. He then grabs the sheet from the helm who returns to the mainsheet and then off they go down the reach. There are variations to this manoeuvre depending on your tactical position at the mark and both the wind and sea states. For example, in the mid to upper wind range and among other boats (when it may well pay to go into the gybe fast and come out high on the next leg of the course), the helm would **not** take the guy and sheet as the crew works the

Good boat balance and trim here for the light conditions. Also good to see the spinnaker trimmer with both the guy and sheet in hand for quick accurate trimming.

pole because he would struggle to keep the boat upright using the mainsheet and less kicker as the crew sorts out the pole first and then fills the spinnaker.

Here is another variation of this manoeuvre. If it is a relatively broad reach free from other boats, go into the mark high, the helm bears away, stands up, takes both guy and sheet from the crew, continues to bear away, ducks(!) and gybes keeping the spinnaker full throughout the gybing manoeuvre. The crew has the option of taking the pole off the mast either before or after the gybe. This is a personal choice, although in the upper winds it is safer to take it off the mast before the gybe as it helps to keep body weight away from the mast area where you don't want it. This helps to keep the bow higher off the water.

Run to run gybe

With only a slight alteration of course, in any boat carrying a spinnaker, the spinnaker should never empty. (If it does, have a quiet word with the trimmer at an opportune moment!) In a dinghy, it is all down to the helm to get it right while the crew deals with the pole. In the larger keelboats, the helm must steer the boat under the spinnaker to assist both the trimmer and the foredeck hand to keep it full.

Key points: Take off the pole, steer underneath the full spinnaker, bear away slightly, roll the boat over to windward and do not let the spinnaker clew too near the forestay. Gybe, continue steering underneath the full spinnaker, crew weight over to the new windward side, reconnect the pole, then carry on at full speed telling the team that they have done a great job! If the spinnaker collapses during the gybe, it is either due to poor trimming or over/understeering the ship through the turn – it is totally down to the trimmer/helm teamwork and normally the fault of the helm for not steering underneath it.

In the dinghies, the helm will take both the guy and the sheet from the crew while standing at the back of the boat keeping the spinnaker full and steering with the tiller between the legs. Then bear away, balance the boat over to windward, the crew looks for the mainsail leech about to move, pulls the main over, brings the boat back upright and then moves the pole. After this he re-takes the guy, puts it back under the reaching hook, or just leaves it through the tweaker/barber hauler and then re-takes the sheet. The helm is then back on to the main and off they go.

A key point for the helm is do not let the spinnaker clew get to the forestay during the gybe. If you do, then it will collapse as the jib will block the air trying to flow into it to keep it full.

A key point for the crew is when it is blowing the dogs off their leads, take the pole off the mast before the gybe, passing it to the new windward side in front of the mast and then gybe. The pole is now in front of you to put straight onto the new guy. This stops you having to go forward round the mast to get the pole off – the last place you want your body weight after a gybe in a breeze!

Spinnaker gybing

Target: Whether it is a broad reach to broad reach gybe, or a run to run, **keep the spinnaker full**. As with any boat-handling manoeuvres, it takes practice so make sure that it is built into your training programme. Teamwork is essential here. In the majority of dinghies, a poor gybe with a collapsing spinnaker is due to a lack of help by the helm who is

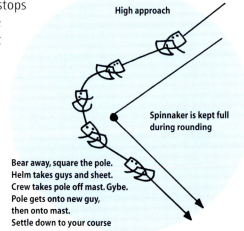

High approach

Spinnaker is kept full during rounding

Bear away, square the pole.
Helm takes guys and sheet.
Crew takes pole off mast. Gybe.
Pole gets onto new guy,
then onto mast.
Settle down to your course

Good to see a sailor acting as a human guy to fill the spinnaker while it's missing a pole.

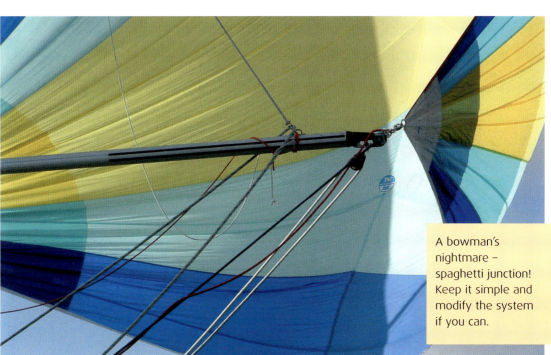

A bowman's nightmare – spaghetti junction! Keep it simple and modify the system if you can.

very often sitting in the back of the boat not doing much! You must be standing with the guy and sheet in hand, steering with the knees and keeping the sail full while the chap at the front is fixing the pole. During training, we spend a lot of time working with racers to get this right as there is much to be gained over those who don't.

Spinnaker drops

The choice is either a windward or a leeward drop, depending on which side you want it next. Dinghies will always do a windward drop, so at the end of a run, be on the correct tack to have it on the right side. So there needs to be forward thinking by the tactical wizard at the back of the ship. Too many times I have seen them coming down either too early or too late. It is all about time and distance to the mark, allowing for both wind/boat speed and, when applicable, tide/current.

Running: Dead easy! Drop the pole in good time, especially in the keelboats, steer under the spinnaker to keep it full. Human guy it! You now have the luxury of either a windward or leeward drop depending upon the words of wisdom emanating from the stern of the vessel!

Reaching: Should you require a windward drop, make a high approach to the leeward mark, bear away and drop to windward. If it is to be a leeward drop, release both the guy and the halyard and bring it into leeward – no problem. In the dinghies, however, we would normally always bring it in to windward as you cannot get down to leeward to do it, especially in the medium to upper wind range.

Key points about spinnaker drops are time and distance: dropping too early when in light winds against a foul tide, or dropping it too late when going with the tide in breeze and continuing past the leeward mark.

Target: Having cleared away everything (including trailing sheets!), you need a nice wide entry into the mark, with a nice exit, close-hauled right next to it – without hitting it!

Always remember to focus on your *own* job in the boat and whenever possible visualise what you are about to do in good time before your reach the mark.

Mark roundings

There is much to be gained and lost during mark rounds, mainly due to your attacking angle to the mark which in turn leads to your exit angle. Do not over-use the rudder or you will lose too much boat speed. Therefore, in order to use less

Good time and distance work, plus good team work in the boat with the kite coming down as the boat rounds the mark.

rudder, you must use your sail trim, boat trim and boat balance to maximum effect to turn the ship.

Windward mark: To bear away, boat balance to windward, boat trim maximum waterline length and further aft in a breeze to lift the lee bow off the water. Ease the main and the kicker and keep the headsail on more to pull the bow off the wind.

Gybe mark: Boat balance to windward, maximum waterline length with your trim, unless it is windy then trim further aft to lift the lee bow. Ease the main to use less rudder during the turn.

Leeward mark: Boat balance dead upright, unless in light winds, then heel to leeward; maximum waterline length with mainsail and jib in together. Boats with large genoas – mainsail on slightly sooner, again to use less rudder during the turn. In the upper wind range, you can balance the boat over to windward during the turn, the boat then coming upright as you bring the sails in during the rounding.

5
Boat Tuning

There are many sailors, past and present, who have that natural instinct for when a boat is feeling good and know exactly when it is going fast through the water. Rodney Pattison, Jo Richards, Eddie Warden-Owen, Jason Belben, Stuart Childerley and many more like them can make a boat go fast in a straight line. So how do they do it? *Mileage, mileage and more mileage*, in the class of boat to be sailed in order to find out what makes it tick, in all wind and sea conditions.

Before any of these guys enters a major event, they will always try to have the best technology around them, with the best possible finish to both the outer hull and foils.

Key boat tuning points:

- **The mast**.
- **Sails**.
- **Boat tuning controls**.
- **Foils**.

The mast

- Have you got the right mast in the boat for the expected sea state at the venue?
- Is it the right mast for your all-up body weight?
- Do the bending characteristics of the mast match the luff curve of the mainsail that you would like to use?
- Does the mast need to be light and soft or heavy and stiff?
- Is the centre of gravity as low as possible?
- Are the fittings on the mast substantial enough to do the job in the upper wind range?

All these questions may or may not be relevant to the type of boat that you race, depending on class rules. Therefore they need to be considered thoroughly when putting a championship campaign together.

Mast heel position

In many classes of boat, the mast heel can be moved fore and aft within class rules, so where does it need to be? The basic guideline for most classes is to go out in a breeze of approximately 4–6 knots, sail the boat close-hauled (ideally the boat should have two to three degrees of weather helm) and when you let the tiller go, the boat should turn slowly towards the eye of the wind. If the boat has more than two to three degrees of weather helm and turns quickly into the wind, then the mast heel is too far aft and

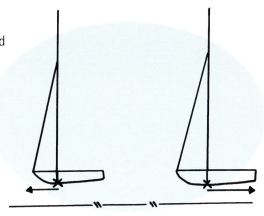

needs to be moved slightly further forward. Should the boat have no weather helm, or worse still lee helm, then the mast heel must be brought a little further aft.

Mast rake

Those classes which can alter their mast rake – from Optimists right up to the America's Cup boats – create an area of great debate and opinions, all of which depend on hull shapes, sail shapes, body weight etc. Optimists can vary from 2.75-2m, the 420 from 6-6.15m and the 470 from 6.6-6.75m. You can imagine the differences in the big boats!

Basic guidelines

The lighter the wind, the more upright is the rig for maximum power. The top of the mast should only be raked more aft as the wind speed increases and the boat becomes overpowered. This allows both the head sail and the mainsail leeches to twist open more easily which reduces the heeling moment of the boat and also reduces weather helm, therefore maintaining boat speed.

Sails

- Flatter water, stronger wind = flatter sails.
- Choppy water, lighter wind = fuller sails.
- Flatter water = firmer leeches.
- Choppy water = more leech twist.
- Firm leeches = power and pointing ability.
- Leech twist = speed.

Never forget this basic boat tuning theory.

It is while racing on flat water, beating to windward, that you can focus on your pointing ability and not worry about waves stopping the boat going forward. It is when an event is held on a flat water venue that the flat water sailors do well. This is because they focus on pointing ability, with flatter sails and firmer leeches and also the use of wind shifts. The sea sailors struggle behind them! Vice versa when the event is on the sea. Then the sea sailors lead around the course, with fuller twisted sails, focusing on working the boat through the waves and not pointing the boat so much. They also make better use of the tide and/or current in relation to lay lines.

Boat tuning controls

- Mast rake.
- Spreaders.
- Cunningham hole.
- Mast ram.
- Kicking strap.
- Barber haulers.
- Clew outhaul.
- Traveller/bridle.
- Centreboard.
- Spinnaker-pole height.
- Rig tension.
- Halyard tension.

Calibrate everything, record everything, mark every sheet and halyard so that you always have the boat tuning foundations with which to work. So much time can be wasted on this variable of our sport, especially in the tactical classes, where the differences in performance lie in the other variables. For the speed machines that only tack once for the windward mark up each beat, this variable takes up a lot of their training programme.

Establish which category you are in, so that you do not waste too much of your time!

Mast rake

If you are not sure of your mast rake settings for a given sea/wind state, ask the class coach or sailmaker for guidance. Failing that, talk to the top sailors of the class. You must get this most basic of boat tuning controls correct for the conditions of the day and be ready to alter the mast rake as the conditions change. On too many occasions in the past, I have seen the conditions change, but this basic boat tuning control not being adjusted – with competitors wondering why their boat speed has dropped off as the race continued!

A good mainsail leech profile for both speed and pointing ability.

INSET: The mainsail is too full and twisted. With the open leech, you cannot point and therefore fall into a lee bow situation with the boat ahead.

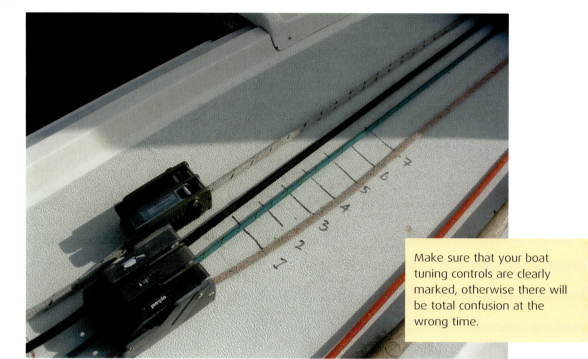

Make sure that your boat tuning controls are clearly marked, otherwise there will be total confusion at the wrong time.

Always be ready to shift gears, as you would in a car, to maintain performance.

Spreaders

In the dinghy world, this is a very important boat tuning control often overlooked to the detriment of both power and speed out of the rig.

Key points
Spreader bracket: Is it strong enough and in the correct position on the mast?

Spreader ends are adjustable at both ends, fore and aft and in/outboard, if class rules permit, and they bisect the angle of the shroud the same both above and below the spreader.

Make sure that the spreader ends do not drop down under pressure. If they do, put a good whipping/seizing below the spreader end to prevent this from happening.

The spreaders are one of the most important tuning controls on the boat. If class rules permit, they need to be adjusted for each race as the wind and sea conditions change. Both the length and angle of the spreader control mast bend fore and aft as well as sideways, having a dramatic effect on the power of the mainsail as well as pointing ability.

Spreader length: The longer the spreader is, the stiffer the mast becomes sideways, as long as the shrouds are being deflected outboard as you look up from the chain plates to the hounds. The shorter it is, the less the mast is being supported sideways and therefore the more it will want to bend to windward at this point. With this theory in mind it is the boats with high aspect ratio jibs, hardly overlapping the mainsail, that need to carry the longer spreaders so that they can achieve maximum power out of the rig. Only the boats with large overlapping genoas will be seen with the shorter length spreaders, allowing the mast to bend at spreader height to windward in order to create a wider slot area between the leeward side of the main and the genoa leech. As the mast bends to windward at this point, the upper section of the mast more readily bends to leeward allowing the upper mainsail leech to twist open, thereby reducing the heeling moment of the boat and reducing weather helm. Basically, as the wind speed increases in these boats, the spreader length decreases, to help depower the rig.

Spreader angle: The further forward the outboard end of the spreader is (that is when you look up from the chain plate to the hounds and the shroud is deflected forward), the more you are supporting the mast fore and aft. This means that the mast is being restricted from bending forwards at this point. This will give you a fuller, deeper mainsail, a firmer leech and maximum power. As you allow the spreader end to come aft, so you are now allowing the mast to bend more forward which allows the mainsail to become flatter and therefore, with less camber in the sail, less powerful. At the same time you are allowing the leech to open more readily which reduces the heeling moment of the boat and the weather helm.

Basically, in the lighter winds you need to set up for maximum power with your spreader ends further forward and, as the wind speed increases, allow them to come further back to depower the rig.

Pre-bent rigs are fast on flat water across the wind range. To achieve this you would set up the spreaders so that, with the rig in tension, the spreader ends are deflecting the shrouds outboard and the shroud itself is a straight line between the chain plate and the hounds. You are now forcing the mast forward at this point, thus creating a flatter mainsail for flat water sailing. This enables you to point higher. If you overdo this you will soon be able to tell by visual diagonal creases running from the spreader area down to the clew of the main. To remove these creases, simply straighten the mast slightly at spreader height.

Good slot shape for both pointing ability and speed. Note the diagonal creases running up from the mainsail clew – a sign of too much pre-bend in the mast depowering the mainsail, especially in light winds and sloppy seas.

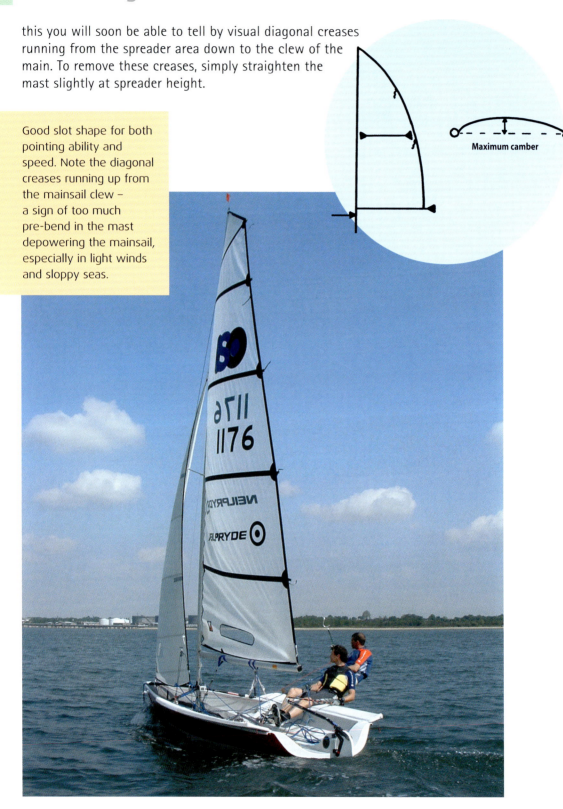

Maximum camber

Pre-bent rigs are fast on flat water/short chop, good for pointing ability and for depowering the rig in the upper wind range.

Cunningham hole

This is probably one of the most underused or forgotten about boat tuning controls and yet it is dramatically effective in achieving both maximum power and pointing ability. This control is far more effective with softer cloth sails such as those found on Toppers, Lasers, HMS *Victory* etc! What is it designed to do? To control the position of the maximum point of camber fore and aft in the sail. Sailmakers place the cunningham somewhere between 40 to 50 per cent back from the leading edge of the sail. As the wind increases over the aerofoil shape, the maximum point of camber is pushed further aft towards the leech. When this happens, the leech returns to windward hooking the mid/lower leech more and therefore creating more heeling moment and drag, plus more weather helm – SLOW!

The basic rules for using the cunningham are as follows:

Light to medium winds: Leave it loose, but as the wind speed increases so does cunningham hole tension in order to bring the centre of effort of the sail back to where the sailmaker designed it to be originally.

In the upper wind speed: Apply maximum tension to try to bring the centre of effort even further forward. This now enables the mainsail leech to really twist open, especially in the mid/upper leech area, and reduce both the heeling moment of the boat and weather helm. As with all basic rules, there may be variations from class to class. For example, in the Laser class I have seen the cunningham hole tension at its maximum 'on' position in light airs, flat water, with maximum kicker set, with a brand new sail and the outcome was a world champion! The theory behind these settings was point high, open the mid/upper leech to create less drag and less weather helm, result gold medal! Moral of the story – always set up for the conditions and never forget your basic boat tuning theory.

Mast ram/chocks

Used to control the amount of fore and aft mast bend at deck level, yet another very important variable in setting up the rig for the conditions of the day.

Basic theory: Light winds, sloppy sea – apply mast ram/chocks to keep the mast straight fore and aft. This will create a maximum power mainsail shape for you to drive through the sloppy, confused sea state. As the wind speed increases and the boat starts to become overpowered, begin easing the mast ram/removing the chocks. This now enables the mast to bend fore and aft, allowing the mainsail to become flatter as well as opening the mid/upper mainsail leech, therefore reducing the heeling moment of the boat, weather helm and drag so that you go faster.

One variation to the light winds setting with which we have experimented in the past is when you are heading straight into a sloppy/choppy sea, keep the mast straight at spreader height for maximum power but leave the mast free to move at deck level. This allows for the rig to flex as the boat is pitching through the waves, therefore not shaking the whole rig to death and losing the wind out of the sails. Something has got to be giving somewhere and deck level movement of the mast fore and aft in these conditions is the answer. Sideways movement at deck level is not desirable in boats with small overlapping high aspect ratio jibs as it will cause both loss of power and pointing ability. However, as the wind speed increases, it is acceptable in the classes with large overlapping genoas in order to allow the mast to come to windward at deck level. This will assist the creation of a wider slot area between the leeward side of the main and the leech area of the genoa, so the wind will escape through the slot area, allowing you to maintain and even increase boat speed.

Kicking strap

This is probably the most important boat tuning control on the boat and sadly, to their cost, overlooked by many both in boat tuning terms and in boat handling skills. The kicker has a great deal to answer for – from approaching the line to start, to boat speed, to pointing ability, to boat stability. The kicker is a power control to the boat. Turn it on/off as and when you require it. A classic example of this is when approaching the line to start in light to medium winds on relatively flat water with no tide/current

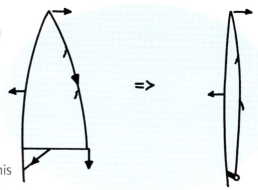

affecting the boat. Many a time, I have seen racers coming to the line too quickly with their mainsails flapping unable to slow down quickly enough to prevent them from being over the line at start time. If only they had popped the kicker off earlier, they would have been OK. What is happening to their boat is, with the kicker in tension, while the mainsail leech is flapping it is driving them forward towards the line. Ease the kicker and they will slow down and even stop going forward.

Elsewhere on the course we see the misuse of this very important boat handling control only too often. If you try to bear away round the windward mark with the tension still on the kicker, in medium to upper wind speed, you will suddenly find that the boat will not turn because the rudder blade is making a gurgle sound and does not want to know! The mainsail leech is overloaded, but if you pop the kicker before you attempt to turn, you will find that the boat responds with much less effort on both the tiller and rudder – again assisting boat speed. Also, while on the reaching leg of the course, especially in the medium/upper wind range, if the kicker is too tight, boats will broach over to leeward out of control. If you are overpowered on the reach, ease the kicker and immediately the boat will become manageable again. The opposite effect of the kicker being too loose during the reaching leg results in the loss of power and boat speed.

On the running leg, the problems are relatively straightforward; the kicker is normally either too tight or too slack. So what do these scenarios bring to the party? If it is too tight in light to medium wind range, you will suffer from a drop in boat speed. If it is too loose in the upper wind range, you will capsize to windward!

Basic theory: In light airs leave the kicker slightly slack with the upper leech flicking open and tighten it as the wind speed increases. The best guideline to determine whether the tension on the running leg is correct is to use your telltales on the upper mainsail leech. They should be streaming off the leech most of the time. If they are stalling too much, then ease the kicker tension.

To windward: Kicker tension while beating varies, not only from class to class, but also in both wind speed and sea state. Basic theory tells us the following key points:

The kicker is too tight here for the wind speed. A little more twist in the mainsail would get the boat going faster downwind.

Open sea/waves require less kicker, so that you have a fuller, more powerful mainsail with upper mainsail leech twist for speed through the waves. To keep the boom on or near the centreline requires more mainsheet tension but you do not want to close the mid/upper leech too much. This is where either the traveller or strop system comes into use. By having them tensioned on the weather side of the centreline, you can maintain mid/upper leech twist and boat speed in waves.

On flat/short choppy water, only in the mid to upper wind range, we now use much more kicker tension to help bend the mast, create a flatter mainsail shape and keep a firm leech for pointing ability. This now requires much more use of the mainsheet by the helm/mainsheet trimmer to ease it in the gusts and bring it back in during the lulls. Hard physical work on the arms – only the fittest will win!

Barber haulers

A critical control used to create the perfect jib and leech shapes relative to the leeward side of the mainsail. This control alone can be the answer to boat speed and pointing ability problems. The barber hauler controls the exact position of the clew of the jib, fore and aft, up and down and sideways – if allowed within your class rules. This particular control must be well calibrated and the headsail sheets marked so that you can relate the mark to the lead block all the time. What are you trying to achieve when setting up this control during a boat tuning session? You are looking to set the barber hauler position so that all three telltales near the jib luff are streaming slightly above the horizontal as you are sailing to windward. If the toptell tale is flying too high, this is telling you that you have too much upper jib leech twist. This is OK for the upper wind speed, but not in the light to medium winds. Therefore, to get the telltale to stream properly, you will need to take the lead block slightly further forward or lower it, whichever option you have on your ship. If the lower telltale is stalling all the time and going around in circles, this signifies that the jib is too full in the bottom, with the leech too hard. Now you need to raise the lead block and/or let it come slightly further aft in order to flatten the lower section of the jib and allow the leech to twist open more easily.

Finally, while beating to windward, if the luff area of the mainsail is back winding too much, this is telling you that the slot area is too narrow (that is the gap between the leeward side of the main and the jib/genoa leech). To open this gap slightly, either

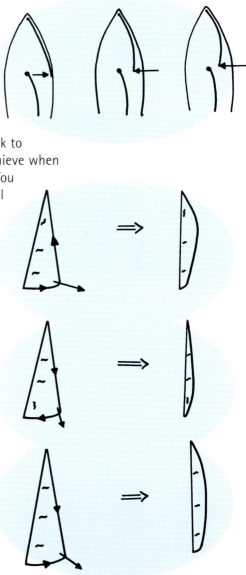

Use of telltales: here the boat is not sailing close enough to the wind as indicated by the leeward telltale not streaming and the windward one stalling – or the sail is over-trimmed for the point of sailing.

raise the lead block a little or take it further aft. If there is no back winding of the mainsail, this is an indication that the slot shape is too open so take the lead further forward and/or lower the lead. What you are looking for, while sailing to windward, is that the luff of the main is just thinking about back winding. If this is excessive your boat speed will be down; if there is no lifting of the main at all, your pointing ability may well be down.

As the sea and wind conditions change, so also must your barber hauler/jib sheet tension so that you maintain boat speed and pointing ability. DO NOT FORGET!

Clew outhaul

This is another control that is often forgotten about, and then racers wonder why they are not pointing, or are slow on the running leg!

The basic theory is as follows:

Singlehanders: Not too tight on the beat as you require the power in the sail low down, as well as wanting the mid/lower leech to return to windward for your pointing ability/power. For both the reaches and the runs, to maintain boat speed,

Good mainsail profile for both speed and pointing ability in the light to medium wind range.

only minor adjustment is required to keep power in the sail and the correct leech shape for the downhill slides. During your early days of sailing in the class, calibrate the clew outhaul position so that you get to know exactly where it wants to be for each point of sailing in the various conditions. Once you have got used to it, you can then remove the calibration if you want to.

Doublehanders: To windward. Clew outhaul should be all the way out to the black band on those boats that can carry a narrow slot area, in the light to medium winds, and/or have headsails where the mid/lower leech returns sharply throwing the wind back into the leeward side of the mainsail. By keeping the clew outhaul tight, you keep the distance between the headsail leech and the leeward side of the main as wide as possible, therefore not stalling the wind trying to get through the gap.

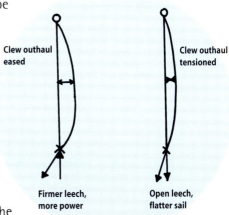

Clew outhaul eased

Clew outhaul tensioned

Firmer leech, more power

Open leech, flatter sail

Once again, downhill on the reach only minor adjustment is required for both power and speed. On the running leg, leave it all the way out to the band to assist upper leech twist in the light to medium winds and to get maximum projection to the wind to maintain boat speed. Only ease it slightly in the upper wind range to assist in closing the upper leech and help to reduce the death roll! Many sailors tend to overlook setting the clew outhaul for each point of sailing, and for the conditions at the time, as it is one of the minor controls. Yet it is so important for power in the mainsail, for pointing ability and all-round boat speed in all points of sailing. So do not forget this when carrying out your mental checklist of things to alter as you turn corners on the race track, or as the sea or wind conditions change.

Traveller/bridle/hoop

There are various options here depending on the class of boat, and personal preference. But the aim is to achieve the same end result, and this is to control the exact position of the outboard end of the boom, the shape of the mainsail leech, and the mast bend fore and aft as well as sideways.

So what are we looking for here? Let us address the traveller set-up first. The traveller is like all the other boat tuning controls – critical! If it is set up wrongly, then speed, power and pointing ability all disappear.

There are three basic settings: to windward, midships or to leeward. When would you want to set it up to windward? While sailing to windward in light winds on the open sea in sloppy conditions. This is when you want maximum power out of the main, with the least amount of mainsheet tension, keeping the boom on the centreline and with a straight mast with mainsail leech twist – FAST!

As the wind speed increases you now want to power the boat up in the medium wind range, keeping the boom on the centreline but firming up the leech more to achieve better pointing ability. To do this, allow the traveller to go down to the centreline of the boat. You now need more mainsheet tension to keep the boom on the centreline which, in turn, firms up the mainsail leech giving the boat more power and pointing ability.

In the middle to upper wind speed, as the boat starts to become overpowered, you now allow the traveller to go down to leeward, to keep the boom end over the leeward quarter of the boat. This requires a good deal of mainsheet tension which, in turn, helps to bend the mast much more fore and aft and only as the boom end is to leeward of the centreline. It also has the effect of bending the mast to windward at both deck and spreader level (the amount depending on spreader length and angle as already explained), as well as the amount of sideways movement at deck level,

If the boat is heeling too much, put more twist in the upper mainsail leech to reduce the heeling moment of the boat. Do this with the traveller more to windward with less mainsheet tension.

if any at all, and the mast section itself (stiffness sideways). All this achieves a flatter mainsail shape fore and aft, as well as more upper mainsail leech twist, to reduce the heeling moment of the boat and the amount of weather helm. Because of the amount of mainsheet tension with the traveller to leeward, the lower leech is still standing firm. This gives both power and pointing ability off the lower leech only, which is exactly where you want it in the upper wind range. The fact that the traveller is to leeward means that the lower leech, although returning to windward because of the amount of mainsheet tension, is in fact parallel with the centreline of the boat and not creating drag and increasing weather helm.

Off the wind, either reaching or running, the traveller can be left on the centreline as the mainsail leech shape will be controlled by the kicker tension. However in some classes, because of the cockpit layout, the traveller is allowed to go down to leeward in order to leave the central area of the cockpit clear. The mainsheet now has more influence on the leech shape as it has more of a downwards component when in tension and so you will need less kicker tension to control the mainsail leech twist.

Bridle/hoop

This is used to reduce the distance between the top and bottom blocks in the mainsheet system, and therefore the amount of rope needed in the boat, thus reducing the all-up weight. For this system to be effective in light winds and sloppy seas, you must be able to tension the windward strop of the bridle so that you can keep the boom on the centreline with the least amount of mainsheet tension. With the hoop system you must be able to pull it up to windward in order to achieve the same thing. In the middle wind range both systems are set up in the middle of the boat and in the upper wind range they are left in the middle. But now you have to play the mainsheet much more in the gusts and the lulls while the kicker controls the leech shape as you ease the boom away from the centreline. The latter seems to work very well on flat water in gusty conditions. As you can see, quite a few variations for the use of either a traveller or a bridle/hoop are very effective in controlling the amount of power in the mainsail and the leech shape for either pointing ability or straight line speed. Make sure that you have it set up correctly for the conditions of the day.

Centreboards/daggerboards

As always, class rules dictate shape, weight, stiffness, materials to be used and flexibility etc. Assuming that you have the best available, with the best finish, what do you do with it?

To windward, light to medium winds: all the way down and in very light winds, when you are maybe trimming the boat down by the bow slightly and if class rules permit, taking the leading edge forward of the vertical helps your pointing ability in these conditions. As the wind speed increases and you have depowered the rig as much as you are able, raise the board slightly and, if possible, angle the daggerboard back a bit to take the centre of effort of the board further aft. This will assist in maintaining/increasing boat speed. This is possible in the Optimist but you cannot alter it backwards in the Laser. How much board do you need up/down on the reaching/running legs? Answer – enough to stand on when you have capsized!

While reaching, you should keep the board down far enough to maintain boat balance, without making too much leeway. If the board is too high while reaching, you can easily suffer from lee helm as well as slipping too much to leeward and ultimately not making the mark. If the board is too far down, you will get the opposite effect of the boat heeling too much to leeward while sailing in the mid/upper wind range, followed by the possibility of a broach and capsize to leeward.

When running in light winds, you can raise the board all the way up with the boat balanced over to windward thereby producing the least amount of drag. Be careful not to capsize to windward! In sloppy sea conditions and light winds, it is better to leave the board down a little to assist better stability. In the middle to upper wind

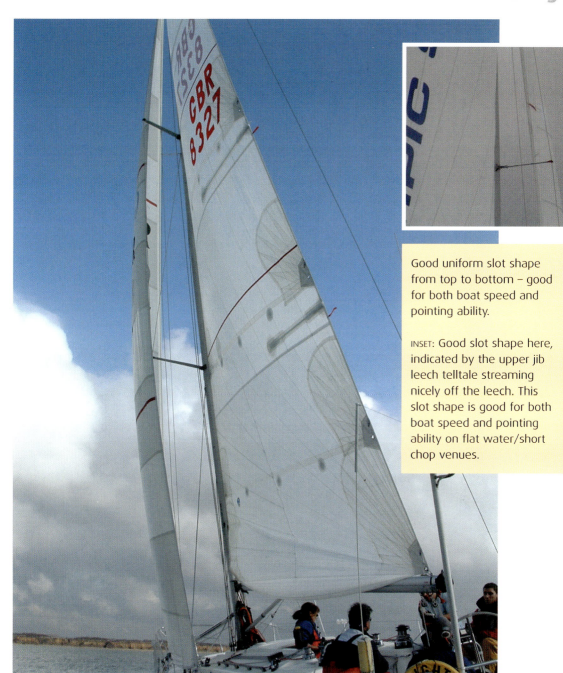

Good uniform slot shape from top to bottom – good for both boat speed and pointing ability.

INSET: Good slot shape here, indicated by the upper jib leech telltale streaming nicely off the leech. This slot shape is good for both boat speed and pointing ability on flat water/short chop venues.

range the board needs to be in the halfway position to maintain stability. If it is too high, you will get the death roll – normally followed by the breaststroke! Likewise, if it is too low, you will trip over it as the water pressure switches from side to side. As you can see, the board position is critical for both boat stability and boat tuning and must be remembered at all times for each point of sailing and the conditions at the time.

Spinnaker pole height

Far too often we see ships legging it off, on both the running and reaching legs, with the spinnaker pole ends at the wrong height for the wind speed at the time. Theory tells us to keep both corners of the spinnaker at the same height above the water while reaching and running. In light winds, while running, this means lowering the end of the pole to keep the two corners at the same height and raising it as the wind speed increases. But you must not raise it too much in the upper wind range otherwise you will not maintain stability. In the upper wind range, if you allow the two corners of the spinnaker to rise too much, the whole centre of effort of the sail becomes too high off the water and has the freedom to oscillate across the bow of the boat more readily – initiating the death role! Now is the time to lower both corners, keeping the sail strapped down and reducing the height of the centre of effort as well as the amount that the spinnaker can oscillate across the front of the bow. Combine this with oversheeting the sail and not allowing the clew to get anywhere near the forestay. This will assist in preventing the sail dragging the boat over to windward and possibly into a Chinese gybe as the water pressure comes onto the weather bow.

Rig tension

On flat water/short chop conditions the rig tension would normally be at its tightest for the following reasons:

- To keep the mast stiffer sideways.
- To support the rig better all round and improve pointing ability.

It is in these conditions that you need to keep the mast as stiff as possible to prevent it from leaning over to leeward, as the boat progresses to windward, thereby improving both the pointing ability of the boat as well as maintaining maximum power out of the rig. As the wind speed increases, and you want to depower the rig, decrease the rig tension to allow the rig to lean over to leeward more which will assist in inducing upper leech twist in both the headsail and the mainsail. As the wind speed increases so does the sea state, more so with the onshore wind. Now is also the time to decrease the rig tension so that the rig will work with the boat as it pitches through the waves while beating to windward. If you head into waves with the rig tension too tight and nothing wanting to give, the whole boat will be shaking herself to death and in most boats this produces poor speed. The same is true when going to windward in light airs in sloppy/choppy seas; something must be giving, so try easing the rig tension as well as not restricting the mast at deck level (for those with deck level supported masts).

It needs good teamwork on the sharp end to perform a quick headsail change. Bear in mind how long it takes to do this, especially if the runway is rapidly getting shorter!

Standing rigging

Cap shrouds: I have explained rig tension – flat water requires tighter rigs, choppy water requires softer rigs. Let us now look at this in more detail. Flat water allows you to put the boat into the pointing mode in all wind speeds. You do not want the rig to be falling over the leeward side while it is going to windward, so the cap shrouds can be at their tightest setting on flat water. The lowers are left relatively loose in order to keep the mast stiff sideways. As the sea state increases, something in the boat needs to be giving so that she is not shaking to death as she pitches through the waves, so now the caps should be eased slightly. This will allow the rig to fall over the leeward side and to flex a little, which absorbs the shock of the boat hitting the waves. As the wind speed increases, use the lowers (Ds) to hold the mast up to windward in the middle, while allowing the top section to fall off to leeward. This helps to open the slot area which is good for boat speed in the waves and is very effective in boats with 100 per cent genoas, ie Dragons, J24s etc. It is interesting to see that the majority of fractional rig boats will go with this configuration as the wind and sea state increase – even those ships with higher aspect ratio jibs, such as Etchells.

Lowers (Ds): On some ships the lowers are in line sideways with the mast and therefore support the mast sideways, keeping it stiff when required, ie light to medium winds on flat water. Allow the mast to bend sideways to leeward in the upper half (to assist upper leech twist) as you become overpowered. Keep the bottom section to windward to assist opening the slot area as the wind speed increases. Some boats have their lowers led from slightly further back. This not only supports the mast sideways, but also allows the mast to bend more fore and aft, as you want it to, on flatter water across the wind range and when you become overpowered as the wind speed increases.

Backstay: The backstay is used to bend the upper part of the mast to depower the head of the mainsail, blading it out as the windspeed increases to reduce the heeling moment of the boat and the weather helm. Only use it as a last resort though, as it is very effective and can lose too much power out of the head area of the main if you are heavy-handed.

Jumper struts: These support the top section of the mast fore and aft and the fullness in the top third area of the main. Set them up firmer when you require a powerful head in the main, ie sloppy and confused sea, light winds. Ease them to flatten off the head while racing on flatter water in any wind speed and also when you become overpowered.

Headsail telltales: You need three pairs, placed in the top, middle and lower part of the sail to ensure that the sail is being trimmed correctly. While yachting along enjoying yourself, because sailing is FUN, all three pairs should be streaming just above the horizontal on the windward side of the sail. If the top one is going

Your top telltale gives critical feedback on power, pointing ability and boat speed. Best guideline is to have it stalling 20 per cent of the time and streaming 80 per cent. In the upper wind range, it should be streaming 100 per cent while going to windward to reduce the heeling moment of the boat.

All halyards must be clearly callibrated for light, medium and strong wind settings so that you can go straight to the mark on the hoist without any guesswork.

more diagonally up in the air, then the lead block needs to go slightly further forward to make it stream correctly. If the bottom one is stalling all over the place, then the lead block needs to go further back to make it stream correctly. The same applies while on the reaching leg.

Halyard tensions: The basic theory is flatter water requires tighter halyards, choppy/sloppy water requires softer halyards. On flatter water, having the halyards tighter helps you to gain a flatter sail shape to put the boat into the height mode. In confused seas, the softer halyards achieve maximum fullness in the sail shape and power through the waves. In your boat tuning logs, it is critical to have recorded all your halyard tensions, not only for the various wind speeds, but also for the sea states. The halyards themselves must be marked for the light/medium/strong wind settings so that they can be set correctly all the time without having to worry about them. On many occasions in the past, as the wind or sea state changes, racers have complained of lack of pointing ability or boat speed. This is normally because they haven't adjusted the halyard to meet the changing conditions.

Boat tuning is a large and sometimes complex subject; that is why the sport is the most challenging in the world! Remember to KISS (keep it simple sailor)! Never forget the basics. If you do, you will then start to go low and slow!

6

Race Strategy

What a great subject. How many times have we seen top racers going fast in the wrong direction? As far as the windward leg is concerned, there are only three options – get it wrong and boat speed does not really matter! You can have the fastest boat in the fleet but if you go the wrong way, you are certainly not going to win any prizes.

Which way to go on each leg of the course is always one of the questions waiting to be answered. Any top sailor would ask this question long before he even arrived at the venue. I think they call it homework, part of your championship preparations!

And of course, when you arrive you need to look closely at the weather and start planning your strategy.

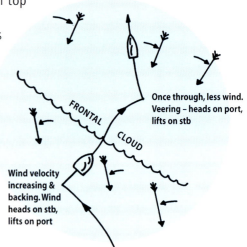

Once through, less wind. Veering – heads on port, lifts on stb

Wind velocity increasing & backing. Wind heads on stb, lifts on port

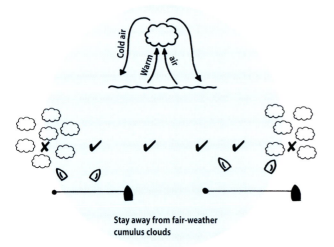

Stay away from fair-weather cumulus clouds

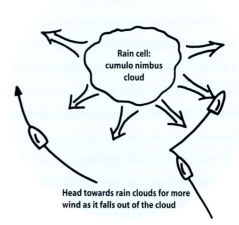

Head towards rain clouds for more wind as it falls out of the cloud

Key things to work on prior to the event:
If you not familiar with the venue, grab a chart or map so that you can start your familiarisation.

Land masses

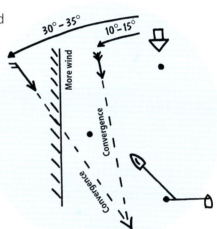

Using your chart or map take a close look at the surrounding land masses and how they will affect the wind direction and strength across the whole of the race area. The height of the land mass also will play a major role in how the wind will behave across the racecourse.

With the land on the port side of the course and the wind direction parallel to it, it pays to go left up the beat for the wind. Why? Because there is more wind on the port side of the course due to the wind convergence area. This increase of wind velocity on the left is caused by the wind over the land mass being more backed over the land – there is more friction over land and less backed over the water, which offers less friction. Therefore, the land wind direction converges with the water wind direction creating a wind convergence area and more wind velocity. Do not forget this basic theory as it will come in handy to give you further answers to land mass scenarios later.

By the way, as and when you have the pleasure of racing in the southern hemisphere, do not forget that the situation there is the other way round. That is, the wind over land is more veered than that over the water so there will be more wind running along a land mass on the starboard side of the course, opposite to that in the northern hemisphere.

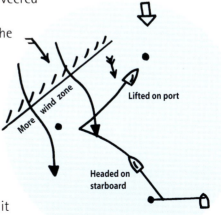

In this scenario, it will still pay to go left up the beat to the wind. Remember the theory already explained above. There will be more wind velocity on the port side of the course. Also, as you head towards the shore line on starboard tack, you will be headed on starboard as you approach the shore, then lifted on port tack along it. All this happens because the wind is backed more over the land than it is over the sea. Also, as wind leaves the land it always tries to do so at right angles to it. Points to remember are:

How far to seaward this deflected wind area will be depends on both the height of the land and the wind velocity. Obviously the stronger the wind and the higher the land mass, the further to seaward will you feel the wind deflection. Also, in this scenario the sea state will be flatter as you approach the land on starboard tack.

When the land mass is at right angles to the wind direction, you are in for an oscillating wind around a mean wind direction, with the windward mark relatively close to the land and the leeward mark approximately 2–3 miles downwind. The breeze will be oscillating during the race and you need to establish pre-start by how much, either side of the mean wind direction, both at the top of the beat as well as in the starting/leeward mark area. What do the top racers do to establish maximum left and right of the wind pre-start? They establish what their headings on both tacks are by sailing the beat. Therefore they know before the start of the race exactly what is high and low on either tack, by using the compass or referring to specific objects on the shore when available.

60°
shifts

20°
shifts

By obtaining this information pre-start, competitors know which is the heading and lifting tack as they try to clear the starting area and therefore which tack to be on initially to take advantage of the wind shifts all the way up the beat. They also use this information to make tactical decisions about positioning, in relation to other boats, so that they can quickly get onto port tack, if that is the lifting tack out of the line. The other piece of vital information that they will have gleaned pre-start is how long it takes for the wind to go from maximum left to maximum right so they have a good idea how long they will spend on each tack before taking advantage of the next shift. What else does this land mass scenario indicate? Well, the maximum left and right oscillation in the starting/leeward mark area will be over a narrower arc and less frequent than it will be in the windward mark area. How frequent and what the maximum left and right is at either end of the course depends on the height of the land and the wind speed. It goes without saying that the higher the land mass is, the wider the oscillations will be, especially in the windward mark area and the lighter the wind is, the more unstable it will be further to seaward.

Other points to remember, given this land mass scenario, are as follows: As the wind leaves the shore to come onto the water, its first sheer in the northern hemisphere is to the right from its backed position over land. Therefore, if the windward mark is close into the shore, you will be lifted on port tack into the mark. Whereas, slightly further offshore, you will be lifted into the mark on starboard tack. The distance offshore depends on the height of the land. Again, establish this information pre-start.

Communication must come from the weather rail calling the wind speed increases and the larger waves.

With the land mass in this position in relation to the race area, it pays to be middle left up the beat for the extra wind velocity. Why? Because there is now less wind up on the top right-hand side of the course, on or near the starboard lay line, if it is close enough to the land. The reason for there being less wind is because there is now a wind divergence area near the shoreline. With the wind over land being further backed than what it is over the water, there will now be two wind arrows diverging along the shoreline, therefore less wind. PROBLEM! Although there will be less wind on the top right of the course, as the wind tries to leave the shoreline at right angles there may well be lifts on starboard tack on or near the starboard lay line. This could be the race-winning move, even though you will be in less wind than those who chose to be middle left up the beat. Check whether or not the starboard lifts are there pre-start

Less wind zone

Diverging wind arrows

and whether or not they will give you the advantage over those who stay further offshore in more breeze. Again, as you approach the land on port tack, the water will be flatter closer to the land – good for both boat speed and pointing ability.

More wind middle left of the course? Why? Answer – there's a divergence zone along the shoreline on the starboard side. The other problem for anyone going to the right is that there is not only less wind, but the wind near the land is also trying to get onto the land at right angles. Therefore this will lift you on port tack as you go into the shore, heading you on starboard as you come out! Not a good picture as you see the opposition crossing ahead on port tack two days away!

The onshore wind gives the most stable wind across the race area, in both direction and velocity. The main effect is in the starting/leeward mark area. If the land mass to leeward is high there is less wind near the shoreline, so as you progress up the beat expect the wind speed to increase. Vice versa as you go down the run – the wind will decrease as you approach the shore, increasing your downwind tacking angles. What is actually happening near the shore is that the wind is leaving the surface of the water to climb up over the land mass. You therefore need to be aware of where this area of less wind is so that you can take the appropriate action from both a tactical point of view as well as adjusting your boat tuning controls, boat trim/balance and sail trim. The sea state will also be more confused in the starting/leeward mark area.

Less wind zone

Diverging wind arrows

Wind most stable in direction & velocity across the race area

Sea breezes

If no gradient wind is present on a morning with a clear blue sky, then this is an early sign for a good sea breeze day, especially if early in the morning there is a light offshore wind indicating that there has been a night land breeze. At approximately 1100 hours, cumulus clouds will start to form over land with no cloud to seaward.

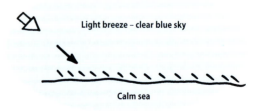

Light breeze – clear blue sky

Calm sea

Downwind, once the boat has settled down, the crew at the front of the ship can assist in looking for the breeze and calling the wind pressure coming down the track.

This indicates that warm air is rising above the land vertically; and as it cools, the clouds develop. As the warm air rises, cooler air above the water is drawn in off the sea to replace it. Thus the circulation of the sea breeze commences.

Initially you will get a local onshore breeze with no wind further to seaward, but as the circulation is completed, approximately 1200–1300 hours, a good sea breeze will fill in from the sea, up to force 4–5. Sea breezes tend to fill in just left of the right angle, ie from 340° on a north coast, 070° on an east coast, 160° on a south coast, and 250° on a west coast. They then stabilise with strength, approximately 20–30° to the right. Later on in the day (1500 hours plus), the sea breeze on all coasts tends to veer and decrease. So always go to the starboard side of the course as the race progresses in order to get the expected veer.

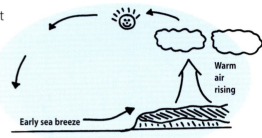

Warm air rising

Early sea breeze

Sea breeze and gradient winds

If a strong gradient wind is present, a sea breeze cannot develop, although locally it can affect the velocity of the gradient wind. If a weak gradient wind is present (less than 20 knots), then a sea breeze can take over, but only as a weak one, for the gradient wind will oppose either the sea breeze circulation aloft or at sea level.

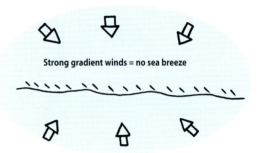

Strong gradient winds = no sea breeze

The basic guidelines are as follows:

If the gradient wind stays at this angle there will not be a sea breeze

A good sea breeze can develop if the gradient wind collapses early in the day. The sea breeze will come from a more veered direction perhaps later in the afternoon.

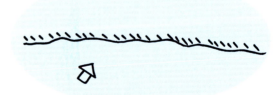

There will be a poor sea breeze, if at all, unless the gradient wind falls below 20 knots, allowing a sea breeze circulation to develop.

There will be a poor sea breeze, if at all, again depending on the gradient wind speed decreasing and the time of day. You could have a light breeze more backed to seaward and more veered closer to the shore.

There will be a poor sea breeze, if at all, if the gradient wind speed is 15–20 knots plus.

Tide/surface current

This is usually either forgotten about, or not enough consideration is given as to how it will affect each leg of the course. How many times have we seen races won or lost through the racer's lack of knowledge on this subject? NUMEROUS!

Before any event, whether it is a sea venue or an inshore lake venue, you need to know all about the tide or surface current, the depth of water and where the movement of water will be stronger or weaker or channelled into a new direction. All this information is gathered by the top competitors prior to the first race – not on the first day of racing – and they talk to the locals, as well as looking at charts. The theoretical knowledge should be put to the test before Race 1 and checked on a daily basis. With this information in place, it could so easily alter your plans in terms of the wind direction in relation to the land mass and the wind speed. Do not forget that the less wind there is, the more important the tide/surface current becomes, especially in slower boats.

The following information is required to establish these key points:

*   Race strategy: which way to go?
*   Starting plan.
*   Lay line calls: beat/reach/run.

Race strategy
The starboard side of the course is favoured for the tide/current on the beat. Stay above rhumb lines for the reaches.

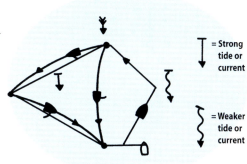

The port side is favoured for the beat; stay low on the reaches. The starboard side is favoured for the run. Which is favoured for the wind? Catch 22!

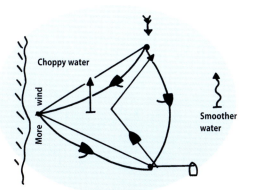

Lee-bow as much as you can. Be above or on the port lay line for the windward mark, above the rhumb line for the first reach, and below on the second reach. Go for the starboard tack on the run, or port tack first, then back on to starboard for a faster point of sailing and better apparent wind.

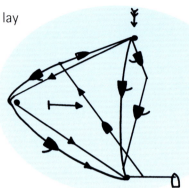

Again, lee-bow as much as you can. Sail above on the starboard lay line, low on the first reach, and high on the second. Gybe to start the run on a port tack or shortly after starting the run for better apparent wind and boat speed.

Go left up the beat and make your final approach above the port lay line. If you can lee-bow the tide or current, then even better – even if you do have to pinch slightly to do it.

Sail above the rhumb line for the first reach, on it for the second reach, and go on starboard tack for the running leg or a short port tack then a long starboard. (It will be vice versa if the tide/current is the same angle from the right.)

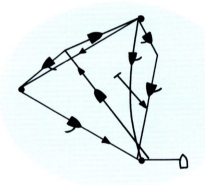

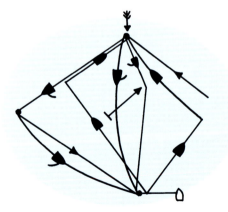

Going left up the beat will give you a shorter port lay line to judge into the mark, tacking just below it. For the first reach you will stay on the rhumb line, and on the second get below it when you can. For the run, make a long starboard tack with better apparent wind (vice versa when tide is same angle from the right).

Starting plan

With the tide pushing people away from the line, look for opportunities to make a good port tack start or a late entry one at the starboard end. Or, with a good transit, a good start out of the middle.

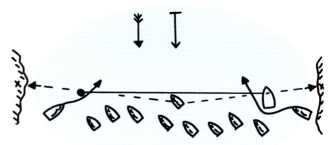

General recall time! Get the best out of the ends. When the one-minute or five-minute disqualification rule comes in, get a good start out of the middle if there is a good transit. Otherwise, stay at one end or the other, depending on which is the favoured side of the beat.

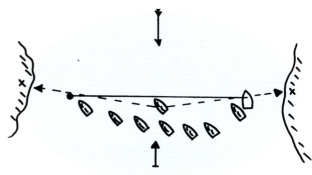

After 'X' general recalls, black flag rule will create a big sag to leeward Grab your chance to be a star!

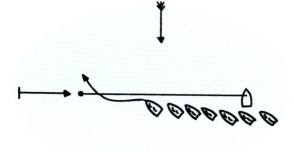

Use the tide to cram the starboard end of the line with more freedom in the port half or quarter of the line.

Use the tide/current to overcrowd and jam up the port end. A late entry could be made at the starboard end if this is the favoured end and/or you wish to go right up the beat.

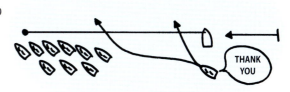

THANK YOU

Summary

Race strategy is a fairly complex subject. However, as long as you take the time to study the theory and then apply it, together with your good boat speed and your ability to point in the right direction, then you should be among the chocolates at the end of the race! To quote a well-used phrase, 'It does not really matter where you are at the start of a race, what matters is where you are at the finish'!

7
Starting

Starting can make all the difference as to how well you do in a race. A good start can mean you've got a 10 per cent chance or a 90 per cent chance of doing well, depending on the course to be sailed and the stability of the wind. If you are racing around the world, then a poor start doesn't matter so much because you have time to catch up and get ahead. But if the wind direction and velocity are stable and the windward mark is only half a mile away, then you've got a 90 per cent chance of doing well if you make a good start. It is amazing how many starts I have done or watched over the years and still the same basic mistakes are being made. To be a good starter, you need:

- ❏ **Determination**.
- ❏ **Concentration**.
- ❏ **Controlled aggression**.

Being in the right place at the right time. Isn't that what life is all about? The top competitors will be in the right place at the right time 90 per cent of the time, having completed all their pre-start preparations in good time. So, what is the thought process that is going through their minds pre-start?

1 Race strategy – which way up the beat?
2 Which is the favoured end of the line?
3 Can you get a transit on the line?
4 Do you want to be at the port end?
5 Do you want to be to windward of the bunch at the port end?
6 Do you want to start out of the middle?
7 Do you want to be to leeward of the bunch at the starboard end?
8 Do you want to be at the starboard end?

All these questions need to be, and are, answered by those who are going to make a good start and their pre-start plan is set before the warning signal. All they have to do then is to execute their plan. Total concentration is now required as they go

Front row clear wind is what the game is all about – could give a 90 per cent chance of doing well in a race.

into the starting period with less than 5 minutes to go. Anxiety levels are at their highest, higher than at any other time in the race – except, perhaps, at the gybe mark in 25 knots of wind! You should be focused on the following key points:

- Positioning – in relation to the line and where you want to be on it (port/middle/starboard end).
- Positioning – in relation to other boats.
- Front row – clear wind.
- Boat handling skills.
- Time and distance to the line.
- Sail trim.
- Racing rules.
- Creating space to leeward.
- Not being sailed over to windward.
- Bow down and accelerating at the right time.

Other factors that come into the starting plan are the wind stability in its direction. If it is an offshore shifty wind, you need to know at start time, as you leave the starting area, which is the lifting tack. For example, if the wind is maximum left as

Numerous competitors here have not concentrated on the start and will not be in the front row in clear wind. DO NOT GIVE UP – re-focus, get on with the rest of the race and recover from there.

you leave the line, you want to get onto port tack as soon as possible. Therefore you do not want to position yourself on the line where you will not be able to achieve this ie at the port end being forced left on a header. You want to be to windward of the bunch at the port end (if it is port end favoured) to stand any chance of getting onto port tack. The same would apply if you wanted to stay on starboard tack on a lift as you leave the starting area. So do not position yourself so that you are going to be forced onto port tack by being lee bowed or by being sailed over to windward.

Most of the top racers look at a starting line in the plan view, then break it down into three parts: port third, middle third and starboard third. They then decide which third to start in, depending on their race strategy plan. Going left = port third, going up the middle = middle third and going right = starboard third. The next decision is where in that third to start? The answer depends on the line bias and your intentions immediately after the start. One of the main aims during the last minute before the start is to create space to leeward so that you can bear away and accelerate at the right time. Quite often you will manage to create the space only to find that another boat comes along and nicks the space that you have worked hard for! It is during this final minute, while creating the space, that you must keep looking behind to see if someone is going to try to steal your piece of water! If they

Second row out of the starboard end of the line, quickly get onto port tack to clear your wind. You will be lifted on port out of the line initially thanks to the deflected wind area around the edge of the fleet.

are, bear away hard, close the door on them, show them that you not going to give it away – they usually disappear further down the line. Be careful to keep to the rules in this scenario!

Line bias

To establish the line bias for the start of the race, use one of the following four methods.

Method 1: Place the boat in the middle of the starting line area and then put her head-to-wind. Look either side of the beam to establish which end of the line (if any) is actually forward of the beam. If one end is, then that is the favoured end of the line from which to start.

This method is quite accurate and can be used on relatively short starting lines in small fleets. However, it is not recommended for long lines and large fleets.

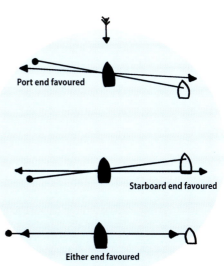

Port end favoured

Starboard end favoured

Either end favoured

Method 2: This is a more accurate method to use. With the mainsail trimmed correctly, reach along the starting line, then tack – without moving the position of the mainsheet – and sail the reciprocal course along the line.

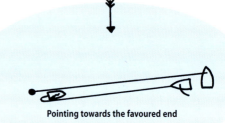

Pointing towards the favoured end

If the mainsail is luffing, or worse still flapping, you are sailing towards the correct end of the line from which to start. However, if after you have tacked and are sailing the reciprocal course the mainsail is overtrimmed and you have to ease it, you are sailing away from the correct end from which to start.

Method 3: The most accurate method is to use your compass. In this example I have first of all taken the starting line bearing 090°. From there you proceed into the middle of the starting line and take a wind reading; in this example, with the boat head-to-wind, the reading is 000°. This tells you that you have a square starting line to the wind direction as it is at a right angle to the wind direction, and so either end of the line is favoured. However, if your wind reading was 010°, then the starboard end would be favoured by 10° as it is 10° closer to the wind direction; and alternatively if the wind direction was 350°, the port end would be favoured by 10°.

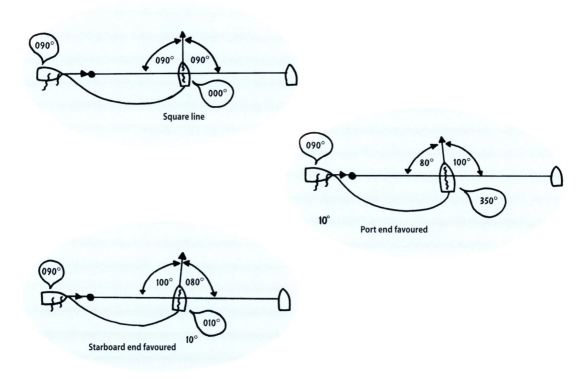

Square line

Port end favoured

Starboard end favoured

> The arm exercise helps the bowman to judge the angles for the line – here he is spot on. Creates great confidence for the afterguard!

Method 4: This method requires the compass and also establishing the tacking angle of the boat on the day of the race. To do this you pre-start tune your boat, check your compass heading close-hauled, tack, and check your heading close-hauled on the new tack. That is your tacking angle.

From this angle you can establish the wind direction – it is halfway between the two closed-hauled compass headings. To see which is the favoured end of the line, first take the line bearing (again in this example it is 090° – from the port end), round the outer distance mark close-hauled on port tack, and then check the compass heading: it is 045°.
If your tacking angle for the day is 90°, then you know that you must be sailing 45° off the wind direction, and so the wind reading in this example is 000°, giving you once again a square line to the wind. If, however, your close-hauled course was 055°, the wind would be 010°, making the starboard end favoured by 10° or, if your close-hauled course was 035°, the port end would be favoured by 10°.

Remember to check your line bearing after the five-minute gun, as up to that time the CRO can alter the line – and many of us have been caught out by this one in the past!

The starting signal has gone, only two boats are on the front row, and even they are well off the line at start time. Time and distance need to be calculated by the rest of the fleet.

Having made a poor start, look for clear wind as soon as possible – tack for it, taking lifts on port tack off the starboard tack leeches.

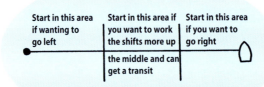

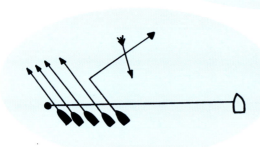 

- If you wish to go right up the beat and the port end is favoured, start to windward of the bunch at the port end in a position where you can quickly tack on to port and go right.

- If you wish to go left up the beat and the starboard end is favoured, always make a port tack approach along the line and tack below the bunch at the starboard end in a position to drive off to the port side of the course.

Port tack approach

Many top racers prefer the port tack approach to the line. Why? Because it gives you more options during your final approach. While hovering on port tack in the starting area, you can sit and watch the start developing whether you are outside the extension of the line at the port end, or anywhere else along the line. By being on port you can also be sailing along the line, behind boats, looking for the gaps to tack into, as well as seeing where the packs of boats are. Stay away from the packs! Top racers do not get involved with a crowd – they are always clear of it, either on the left or the right, so that they have the freedom to manoeuvre after the start in clearer wind.

Transits

Whenever possible, always try to find a good transit on the line for all the right reasons. It will assist you in judging exactly where the line is, especially when you want to start out of the middle on either of the penalty flag starts. When the black flag penalty start comes into operation, now is the time to use your transit to great effect as the fleet normally becomes very line shy, as they also do in the wind with tide scenario. You can get the perfect start in clear wind by using your transit with confidence. Do not forget to check your transit after the preparatory signal as the Race Committee can move the line up to that moment.

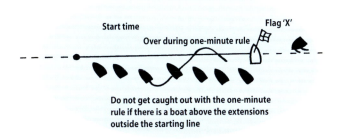

Do not get caught out with the one-minute rule if there is a boat above the extensions outside the starting line

At any National, European, World, or Olympic championship, starting plays a major role in your success and the end result. You can ask any of the top racers and they will tell you that. The only time that you may get back into a race after having made a bad start is when the wind is unstable in both strength and direction and/or if there are gains to be made by the use of either a surface current or tide, which the opposition has failed to capitalise on. **PRACTISE – PRACTISE – PRACTISE**, until you are happy and confident in both your starting techniques and ability.

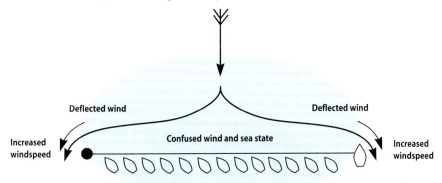

8

Tactics

This book is not specifically about tactics – there are plenty of those available today. However, there are some tactics that always seem to crop up around the racetrack, where the same mistakes are continually being made. These are at the following scenarios:

- ❏ **Starting area**.
- ❏ **First beat**.
- ❏ **Windward mark**.
- ❏ **Run**.
- ❏ **Leeward mark**.
- ❏ **Beat**.
- ❏ **Reach**.
- ❏ **Gybe mark**.

All these different parts of the course require decisions to be made so that you place your ship in the right place at the right time, in order to gain the advantage.

Good to see clear instrumentation for both the skipper and the tactician. Make sure that it is always correctly calibrated!

Starting area

The main tactical mistakes here are:

- Positioning yourself too close to the boat to leeward.
- Leading towards the port end with the tide behind you, getting there too early.
- Trailing in at the starboard end with the tide against you and being squashed out.
- Starting in a crowd and not having the freedom to move after the start.
- Sitting on starboard tack hovering for too long, thereby closing down your options.
- Being at the port end, not making the line and having to gybe out of it with less than 30 seconds to go.
- Not positioning yourself on the line where you would like to be so that you can execute your race strategy plan.

You need to address these mistakes in your training programme so that you have all the answers on race day.

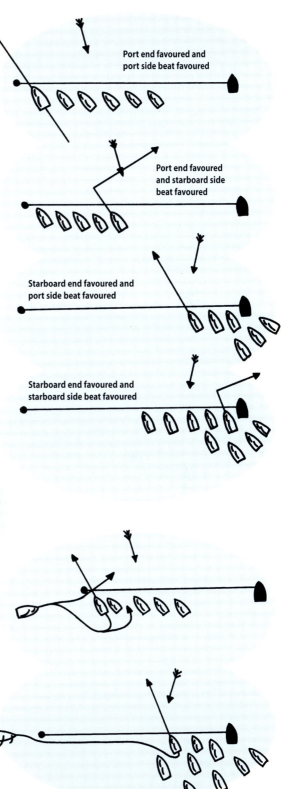

Port end favoured and port side beat favoured

Port end favoured and starboard side beat favoured

Starboard end favoured and port side beat favoured

Starboard end favoured and starboard side beat favoured

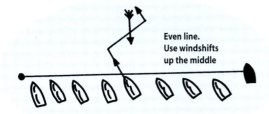

Even line. Use windshifts up the middle

Many top sailors will consider making a port tack approach to the starting line, therefore keeping their options more open.

By approaching the line in this way, you get a much clearer view of how the start is developing, and you will encounter less hassle from other boats and from the rules.

First beat

Having made a good start, what do the
top racers now strive to achieve tactically?
Answer – **to stay between the
majority and the next mark!**

START – CONSOLIDATE – WIN!

The main tactical mistakes are:

* Getting detached from the majority of the fleet when not certain that you are
  going the right way!
* Sailing in dirty wind.
* Being forced the wrong way up the beat.
* Coming into the windward mark on port tack, when the rest of the world are
  arriving on starboard!
* Overstanding the mark due to lack of knowledge about the surface current or tide.

Are you on a lift or a header at the moment?
If you are on a lift, stay on course; if you are
on a header, perhaps you should tack.

How are you doing in relation to the rest
of the fleet? Are you between the majority
and the windward mark?

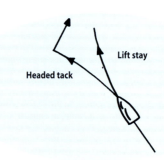

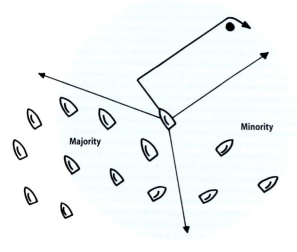

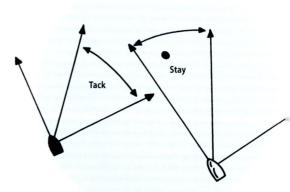

Are you on the tack taking you closest to the windward mark?

Points to consider on the windward leg: If you want to cross the race area because of either a persistent wind shift, or to consolidate your present position and gain on the opposite side of the beat, then always try to cross the windward leg of the course in the middle where there will be fewer boats and less confused wind and water.

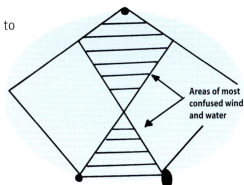

Areas of most confused wind and water

Windward mark

Many tactical errors are made at the windward mark, especially at the end of the first beat while the fleet is still tightly packed. Key mistakes are:

*   Approaching below the lay line, having to shoot it because you cannot tack, not making it and subsequently hitting the mark. Fatal! Make sure that your final tack is such that you can make the mark, allowing for any surface current or tide.
*   Approaching on port tack when it is obvious, from well back, that you are not going to get round. Be like a chess player – think ahead!
*   Remember there are racing rules that apply to rounding the mark. If you are close-hauled on port tack, with a boat close but clear astern, leaving the mark to port, as the boat clear ahead you may not be able to tack without infringing a rule. Be prepared to slow down in order to force the boat clear astern onto your starboard side, so that you can now tack round the mark. If you are making a port tack approach, make sure that your final tack to round the mark is completed outside twice the hull length of the mark, so that you do not infringe a rule.

Tack for clear air and stay on port tack if port is lifting or if the starboard side is favoured. Or, bear away at speed for clear air to leeward, if you are on the lifting tack or are laying the next mark with a long way to go to it.

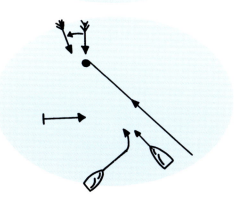

Tack below if you can lay the mark (marks to port), or if the tide/current is taking you from left to right and you are just below the lay line, or if you favour the port side of the course for either a favoured tide/current or an expectant backing wind shift. Bear away and take the opposition's transom for all other options.

Sail the opposition on to guarantee your position, whether you are leaving the mark to port or starboard. This also applies if you are on port tack on the starboard lay line.

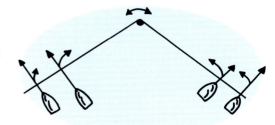

Call for water to tack to gain the advantage and a place. If you do not, and you bear away, you will have to give room to the boat on your weather quarter to clear the starboard tack obstruction as well. You will therefore lose the opportunity of gaining a place.

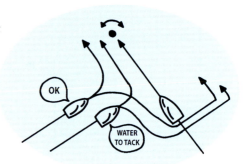

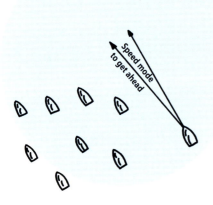

While high on a group of boats to leeward and in a lifting wind shift, go for speed and not for height – especially if you are next expecting a header with a backing shift. This works well in high-performance planing dinghies, but not in heavier displacement boats.

Tight cover or loose cover – boat to boat or boat to group covering situations are always occurring, and you must be prepared to take the appropriate action.

Tight cover: You would place a tight cover on an opponent if you wished to: (a) slow them down, or (b) force them to tack off.

Loose cover: You would put a loose cover on an opponent if you wished to encourage them to continue on their present course because you believe it to be the correct way to go up the beat with the majority of the fleet.

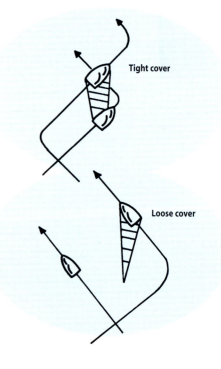

Here the boat is falling into the dirty wind of the boat ahead. The tactician of the boat on the right must be looking to tack as soon as possible for clear wind.

There will also be times when you will wish to do a dummy tack to trap your opponent and force them to tack; this will once again slow them down by making them do a double tack. Likewise, as the attacking boat from behind, you can also throw in a dummy tack in order to try to break cover.

You should not be on the lay line, far from the mark, with boats coming in and tacking on you, ahead of you or under your lee-bow.

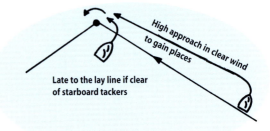

High approach in clear wind to gain places

Late to the lay line if clear of starboard tackers

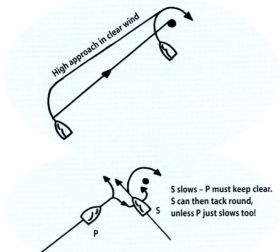

High approach in clear wind

Here, the boat on starboard tack can slow down and force the port-tack boat to do one of two things: (a) take his stern and therefore not make the mark, or (b) tack off for the starboard tack boat, giving him more of a lead.

S slows – P must keep clear. S can then tack round, unless P just slows too!

Summary: These are just a few of the most common situations in which you are likely to find yourself while sailing the windward leg. Always try to keep calm, think positively about your next move(s) and keep clear wind at all times. Also, never forget your basic race strategy before executing your moves.

Run

The most basic mistake:

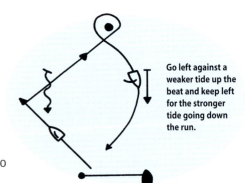

Go left against a weaker tide up the beat and keep left for the stronger tide going down the run.

- Going the wrong way! Before rounding the mark, you must have decided which will be the fastest way down the run for all the right reasons – WIND, TIDE, WAVES. Having made this decision, you will now either bear away or gybe to start the running leg.
- Tactically, stay between the opposition and the next mark.
- Keep your wind clear as the defending boat.
- Always try to sit on the opposition's wind when attacking. When they gybe, so you gybe inside them and on their wind again in order to reel them in.

- While defending, many racers forget to continue to sail the boat fast using both the gusts to soak off to leeward, as well as the lulls to come up and maintain boat speed. Keep using the waves to stay ahead of the game.

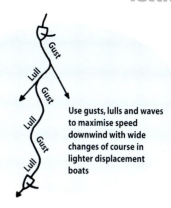

Use gusts, lulls and waves to maximise speed downwind with wide changes of course in lighter displacement boats

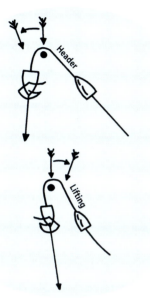

If high on starboard tack when approaching the windward mark (marks to port), gybe immediately.

If low, bear away first.

On short running legs, as a leader, stay outside the blanket wind zone to maintain speed over those trapped in the zone, then cut in on a faster point of sailing at the end of the run.

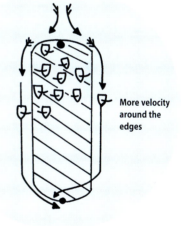

More velocity around the edges

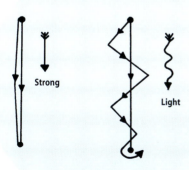

Generally speaking, the stronger the wind, the flatter you can sail down the run (straight down the rhumb line). In light winds you will have to sail slightly higher to maintain speed; this is more pronounced in catamarans and the heavier keel boats.

When leading, stay between the opposition and the leeward mark whichever way they go.

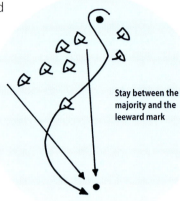

Stay between the majority and the leeward mark

Towards the end of the leg, and if close to others, start looking for the overlap(s) and the inside berth when rounding the mark. Don't forget to allow for different angles of approach by other boats when establishing overlaps.

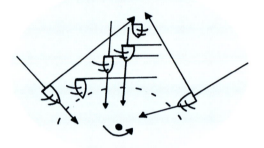

To make the best rounding at speed, the final approach to the mark should be wide and must be on the correct tack with a narrow exit from the mark.

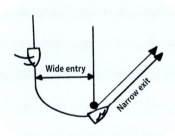

Wide entry

Narrow exit

Gybe inside and on top all the time to close the gap

As an attacking boat from clear astern, in order to close the gap this vessel must gybe on top of the leader all the time to take their wind and also to try to make them make a mistake. Making this leg last longer improves their chances of closing the gap and getting an overlap at the leeward mark.

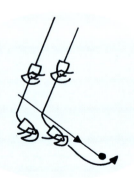

Using the rules, take the opposition out to the lay line before gybing and securing your inside berth, or be clear ahead as you round.

Remember to stay between the opposition and the next mark.

Summary: Running tactics are equally as exciting as on any other leg of the course. Think about your options and grab the chances as and when you can. These situations do tend to develop very quickly, so – like a good chess player – always be a few moves ahead in your mind to gain the advantage at the right time as the opportunities arise.

Leeward mark

The most common mistake is taking the wrong angle of attack. To make the best rounding, pass the mark close-hauled, just missing it and allowing for any tide/surface current. You must always try to make a wide approaching angle, with the narrow exit angle, not the handbrake turn at the mark which people normally do – leaving a gap big enough for a double-decker bus to drive through!

- Being on the outside of one or more boats while in the rounding manoeuvre is another tactical mistake. Again, foresee this development, slow down, let those

Do not make this mistake. Allow for the tide taking you below the starboard lay line.

ahead of you make the mistake while you make the better rounding and gain heaps on those who did not.

- Approaching the last third of the leg, many make the mistake of not positioning themselves ready to protect the inside berth at the mark and therefore having the advantage. Keep up with that forward thinking like a chess player!
- Do not gybe at the mark because this will give you a bad leeward mark rounding.

Additional errors:
- Not staying between the majority and the windward mark.
- Not positioning yourself on the track correctly from a race strategy point of view, in relation to either one boat or a small group of boats.
- Not sailing your own race but spending too much time looking outside your own boat. LOOK FORWARD – GO FORWARD!
- Not shifting gears to meet the changes in either wind speed or sea state.
- Not focusing enough on both boat balance and boat trim.

Reaching

Common mistakes here are:

- Not protecting your wind.
- Getting too low in gusty conditions, allowing boats to roll over the top.
- Not allowing enough for the tide/surface current, sailing the great semicircle.
- Approaching the gybe mark too high, allowing those who went low to gain the advantage, as they approach with speed and the inside overlap.

Check your compass course for the reaching legs. This should be 135° from the windward leg (assuming that the gybe mark is set with a 90° angle).

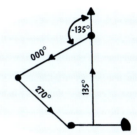

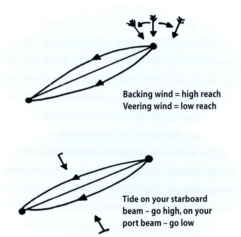

Backing wind = high reach
Veering wind = low reach

Tide on your starboard beam – go high, on your port beam – go low

Check whether the wind direction is relatively stable or whether it is steadily backing in accordance with the weather forecast. If it is backing, first go high down the reaching leg above your compass bearing. If the wind is veering and expected to go right, go low below your compass bearing.

Check what the tide or surface current is doing and be ready to allow for it while pounding down the reaching leg.

As on any leg of the course, you must keep clear wind. The worst situation to be in is when you know that, for either wind or tidal reasons, the fastest way to go down the reach is below the rhumb line; but you also know that immediately behind you is a bunch of boats that, as soon as you go low, will sail over the top of you – taking your wind like one mass blanket. In this situation you must protect your wind first and stay between the opposition and the next mark.

Defend your wind first and go low when you can

You will only have the freedom to sail your preferred course downwind when there is a significant gap between yourself and a group clear astern. This is equally true when reaching in gusty conditions. Never go low and allow the opposition to get high, catching the gusts before you and subsequently rolling over the top of you.

Bear away in the gusts and come up in the lulls for maximum speed down the reaching leg.

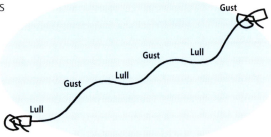

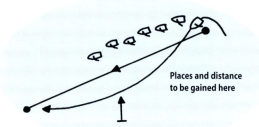

Places and distance to be gained here

If behind a leading group, take the opportunity to go low early to gain places towards the end of the reach.

If clear ahead, make a high approach to the gybe mark to facilitate a good rounding.

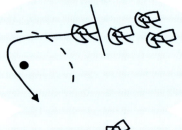

To gain the advantage on the next leg, try a crash gybe and go high as soon as possible.

At the start of the second reaching leg, stay on starboard tack to use the backing wind and the tidal direction.

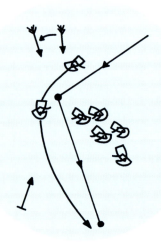

As the leading boat, be aware of the Racing Rules.

Proper course

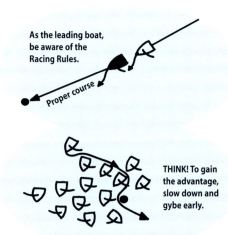

THINK! To gain the advantage, slow down and gybe early.

Gybe mark

Tactical errors here include:

- Not making a high approach when in a position to do so, followed by a slow even turn, exiting the mark close on the new tack.
- Handbrake turns at the mark with the spinnaker ending up between the mast and the forestay!
- Rounding on the outside of one or more ships. Slow down, let them go ahead and come inside so you are above them in a better attacking position to begin the next leg of the course.
- Not assessing whether the next leg of the course is a tight or low reach. If high, you must position yourself so that you can get high as you exit the mark. If low, you must break away low as soon as possible to gain during the last 50 per cent of the leg going into the leeward mark.

All the above-mentioned scenarios are those that are most commonly overlooked or not given enough consideration when progressing around the course. Being focused and thinking ahead is the only way to be a good tactician. Never forget that everyone makes mistakes, even the winner, but not as many as the boats finishing second and third and so on down the fleet. Identify your tactical mistakes, talk about them after each race and eliminate them from your programme.

Always protect what you have got tactically. If seemingly down the pan and round the 'U' bend, look for opportunities to gain from a race strategy aspect, either a change in wind direction or tidal advantage.

NEVER GIVE UP.
NEGATIVE THINKING brings NEGATIVE RESULTS.
POSITIVE THINKING brings POSITIVE RESULTS.
Do not forget, you are not going to do well
in every race!

9 Racing Rules

Although this is not a book about the Racing Rules I think it is important to note the following. Generally, the standard of knowledge of the Racing Rules in Great Britain is pathetic! Why? Answer – because at club level of racing, we tend not to bother with them; it's a case of, 'Sorry about that, I'll buy you a pint afterwards!' At the time of the incident, we are often unsure about who is right or wrong and if there is no protest we do not learn from our mistakes. Then we start attending open meetings and competing in National Championships and continue in the same frame of mind. It is at club level where we really need to learn the rules so that when we progress to the higher levels of racing, we know what we are doing and what we are talking about! On numerous occasions, I have been astonished at the lack of knowledge on this subject. I have actually been to a world championship where a GBR competitor had never previously been in front of a protest committee, let alone an International Jury!

Knowledge of the Racing Rules is a high priority for those who wish to be successful in the most challenging sport in the world. Start learning them thoroughly at club level of racing, and consult *Paul Elvstrøm Explains the Racing Rules of Sailing 2005–2008* and *The Rules Book 2005–2008* by Eric Twiname, revised by Bryan Willis (both published by Adlard Coles Nautical, www.acblack.com). Take every opportunity to sit before a protest committee so that you can learn from the experience, find out what to expect when you sit in front of them, learn about protest procedures and discover what sort of mistakes you may make and how to avoid them in the future.

While hoisting the spinnaker as the windward boat, be careful not to infringe the rule. GBR 5615 (far right) needs to give herself the room to keep clear.

Do not try to force a passage if you were clear astern at the two-boat lengths zone. If you do, you will be given a penalty or be disqualified if this goes to protest.

While on port tack, keep a good look out and be prepared either to bear away or tack to avoid any starboard tackers. Remember not to infringe the tacking rule while tacking!

The Racing Rules are both your attacking and defensive weapons of the sport. Your superior knowledge in this subject can be the difference between a gold or silver medal at all levels of the sport.

Learning curve: Learn the Racing Rules in the following order:

- ❑ **Fundamental rules**.
- ❑ **Definitions**.
- ❑ **Part 2**.
- ❑ **Part 4**.
- ❑ **Part 3**.
- ❑ **Part 5**.
- ❑ **Part 6**.
- ❑ **Part 7**.

Never forget Racing Rule 91 (always buy your coach a drink!).

Make sure that when clear astern you allow for the spinnaker not touching the backstay of the boat clear ahead. If it does you will take the penalty for not keeping clear as the boat astern.

10 Protests

There is nothing nasty about lodging a protest. In fact if you do not protest when you should, then you are bringing the sport into disrepute because someone is going to get a result when maybe they should not, which is not good for the overall results of the event. When I crewed for Lord Nelson in the good old days, it was a 'self-policing' sport which worked very well. The sailors policed it very well either by taking their retirement and/or protesting or, as in more recent years, taking their penalty. It is very sad to see that this past ethos of the sport has declined to the degree that, at many events, we now need 'on the water policemen' which come at great expense to the organising authority.

In my opinion the time has come when we should once again police ourselves to a better degree while racing. Do you need to have a collision before you break a racing rule? Answer: No! How do you lodge a valid protest? Answer: By hailing one word, 'Protest', and nothing more. Shouting 'do your turns' is meaningless. Having hailed 'Protest', forget it and re-focus on your race and continue with it. If required, immediately fly your *conspicuous* protest flag. If you do not fly your flag when it is required, you will not have a valid protest. As soon as you reach the shore, 'leg it' to the race office, collect your protest form, find out the deadline for protests, fill out your form and hand it in on time. The sooner you do this the better it will be for you if there are numerous other protests arising from the race. Otherwise you could find yourself hanging around for ages.

When filling out your form, the advice is to draft it in rough before writing the final copy. Ensure that it is filled out to the best of your ability, neatly and with all the requirements as per the rules met, ie identifying those involved, the incident and the rule(s) which you consider to have been infringed. Your drawing of the incident should be over three separate positions, if applicable, the first one showing the start of the incident, followed by position two and then three, the point where the incident took place. Having handed in your form, in time, find out when the protest will be heard. Once you know this, prepare yourself for the hearing.

When lodging a protest, make sure you identify the right boat.

If you can, eat and drink beforehand, especially if it is going to be a long wait. Turn up at the hearing looking smart – No, not in a DJ but neither in shorts, T-shirt and flip flops! First impressions created as you walk into a protest room can count in terms of your overall impression on members of the jury/protest committee. Whether you are the protestor or protestee, first impressions do count. Do not forget that you are in a fifty-fifty scenario. Enter the room with confidence, not cockiness, with your rule book, note book and pen in hand. At the very least, try to give the jury the impression that you know what you are doing and might know what you are talking about! During the hearing, speak when spoken to, do not try to teach the jury or, worse still, give them the impression that you think that they do not know what they are talking about! Do not interrupt anyone. When presenting your case, initially position the model boats being careful to put them in exactly the right place in relationship to each other and the mark, if applicable. Once in position, take your hands away and state your case before then re-positioning the models. Again take your hands away and talk about it.

It is best to present your case in three stages, if applicable, being careful not to use words like, 'maybe', 'not sure' or 'think so'. Words have to be positive and clear and the less you say the better! When both parties have presented their evidence, do not forget that the protestee has the last word in summing up and that it could change or sway the jury's thoughts favouring one over the other right at the end of the hearing, so be aware of this. At the end of a hearing, win or lose, shake hands both with your opponent and the jury. That will go down well with the jury ready for your next meeting with them wherever that might be in the world. The same applies even at club level, as you may well be seeing them again if not in the protest room, then maybe in the bar!

11

Compass Work

As the kicking strap is probably the most important boat tuning control in the vessel, so the compass is probably the most important tactical piece of equipment in the boat.

Over the years, I have been amazed at the number of sailors who either did not know how to use a compass when racing, or have felt that they did not need to know how to use one. This has usually been the case with sailors who have mainly raced in landlocked areas. Unfortunately, when these people then have to race on open sea venues for their National, European or World Championships, they cannot understand why they sometimes don't have very good results. Often the reason for this is because they lack the knowledge of how to use a compass to establish the following key points in the race area:

- **Race area orientation**.
- **Tacking angle for the conditions**.
- **Wind shift tracking**.
- **Transits**.
- **Wind shifts to windward and running**.
- **Wind bends**.
- **Course leg bearings**.

Race area orientation

When you are racing on an open sea venue anywhere in the world you will find it very useful to take to sea with you a scaled-down chart of the race area in a waterproof laminated sheet. Once the race course has been established by the Chief Race Officer, you can take a fix using your compass to position yourself on the chart. When you know exactly where you are, you can establish your position in relation to deep/shallow water; strong/weak tides; tidal direction; and how wind bends may affect you from surrounding land masses. This knowledge could be the difference between a gold or silver medal, and could psychologically give you more confidence to do well in the race. It is well worth doing at important national and international events. If and when you are coach-supported at an event, this will all be done for you. Your coach will have the relevant information ready to pass on to you when you arrive at the race area.

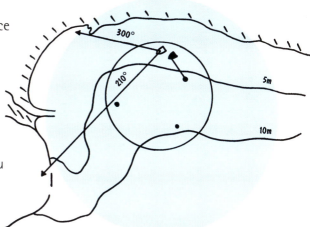

Tacking angle for the conditions

You must use your compass to work out your tacking angle for the conditions of the day. This will assist you in establishing the following key points:

- Wind direction.
- Wind shifts.
- Lay line calls on the beat.

It is important to remember that as both wind speed and sea state change, so will your tacking angle. Generally speaking, the flatter the water, the narrower your tacking angle will be, and vice versa as the sea state increases.

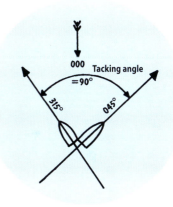

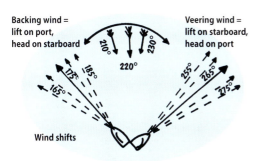

Wind shifts

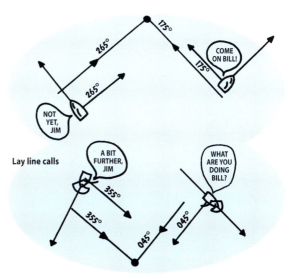

Lay line calls

Wind shift tracking

This is an important part of pre-race preparation in order to establish the following key points:

- What is the wind direction at present in relation to the daily prediction?
- Is there an oscillating wind direction?
- Is there a steady wind direction?

While in the starting area, wind shift tracking should take place for a period of at least 20 minutes to establish exactly what the wind is doing before the start. If the sea state is relatively flat, this can be done by putting the boat 'head-to-wind' and holding her there for approximately 30 seconds. If, however, the sea state is choppy, it is better to sail close-hauled on either tack; by knowing your tacking angle this will give you the wind direction. This should be done every few minutes in order to develop your wind shift tracking chart.

Knowing what the wind direction is at start time, and what it may do next as you come off the starting line, is your ace card. This could make the difference between being among the 'chocolates' at the first windward mark or not!

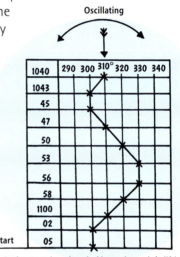

At the start time the wind is maximum left, lifting the port tack, and is expected to go right next

Transits

Your compass is also put to good use to establish a transit along the starting line if and when you cannot achieve a good transit with an object on the shore. With this compass bearing of the starting line you can now sail along the line confidently, allowing for any tide/surface current knowing that you are on or near the line approaching start time. Make sure that you allow a little extra safety margin should the one-minute rule be in force.

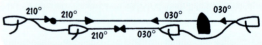

Wind shifts to windward

Sailing at a venue with an oscillating breeze, or one with a natural wind bend over the race area, is when the compass comes into its own and helps to ensure that you are going to be among the 'chocolates' at the windward mark. Having established your tacking angle during your pre-start preparations, you know what your compass headings are on both port and starboard tacks. From the data gathered from your pre-start wind shift tracking chart, you also know which tack is your freeing tack off the starting line.

Immediately after the start, your first tactical move is to ensure that you are on the lifting tack. If that is port tack, then make sure that your positioning on the start line allows you to get onto port as soon as possible having cleared the line, unless you have been able to start on port tack (very rare in the bigger fleets). Now that you are on the lifting tack and have settled down, you are looking for the expected header. While sailing on starboard tack, a minus reading indicates the header, while on port tack it is a plus reading; and as this happens, so the appropriate action is taken. If the shifts are fairly frequent, then it would be advisable to tack straight away, whereas if you thought it was heading you into a wind bend it would be better to carry on a little further to take full advantage of the bend.

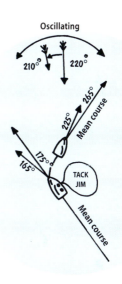

Wind shifts on the running leg

As you approach the windward mark, you know whether you are on a lift or a header; this tells you whether or not to bear away or gybe to start the running leg so that you are in sequence with the wind shifts downwind. Using your wind indicator, you can now detect the shifts downwind so that you are not sailing by the lee.

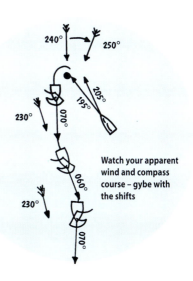

Watch your apparent wind and compass course – gybe with the shifts

Wind bends

Pre-start you will use your compass to detect a natural wind bend over the race area (these are normally found in bays). Sail the windward leg on either tack, and as you progress to windward you may see that you are either being lifted/headed steadily. This tells you that you are sailing in a wind bend created by a natural surrounding land mass.

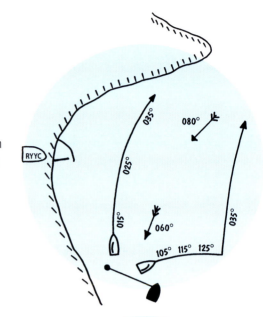

Course leg bearings

It is important for you to know the course leg bearings once the race management team have designated the windward mark bearing, just in case visibility becomes poor during the race or the marks are not very conspicuous. Many a time I have seen the leading boat head off in the wrong direction on either the reach or running leg and others have followed!

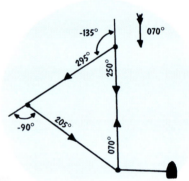

Positioning of the compass

Only one compass is needed in the boat; this keeps down the all-up weight and expense. It should be positioned well forward in the boat to keep your angle of sight as narrow as possible between compass, telltales and waves.

Summary

As stated at the beginning of this chapter, the compass is very important; and to succeed in the sport in the future it can only be advantageous to learn how to use one. In our youth training we teach 11 to 12-year-olds how to use one at Optimist/Cadet level – so that the compass becomes functional in the boat and not just something to 'psych out' the opposition in the dinghy park, or something in which to keep your pet goldfish!

12 Race Management

Knowledge of race management is part of your race training programme. What we do not want to see, when a Race Committee either flies a signal or makes a sound signal, is competitors scurrying to ask their coaches what they mean! Know your flags and their meanings. Never be caught out by your lack of knowledge and awareness of what the Race Committee is doing. The most common error made by competitors is sailing too far away from the committee boat when they are flying the Answering Pennant (AP). When the AP comes down, you have one minute before your five-minute warning signal so you must be within both visual and hearing distance and allow for where you want to be on the line, especially in tidal conditions and light winds. So whenever the AP is flying I would advise that you stay near the committee boat! Be aware of all three penalty flags and their meanings. Check in the sailing instructions whether or not they have been amended. Be fully aware of the meaning of Flag 'Z'; you will be amazed how much difference 20 per cent can make to a podium position on the last day of racing!

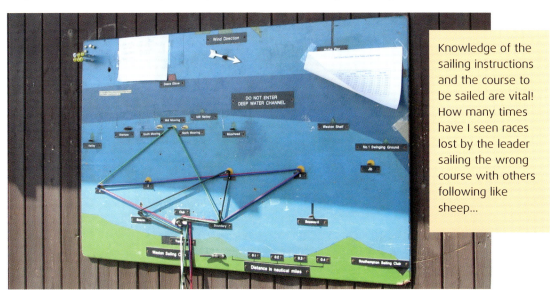

Knowledge of the sailing instructions and the course to be sailed are vital! How many times have I seen races lost by the leader sailing the wrong course with others following like sheep...

When the AP is flying, do not get too far away from the committee boat.

Race management and sailing instructions go hand in hand, so please ensure that you are fully aware of the sailing instructions and their meaning. Whenever possible you should take a set afloat with you for reference. I wish I had a pound for every time I have seen the leader take off on the wrong course and others follow, at both selection trials and world championships.

There will be occasions when the Race Committee does things with which you disagree. Forget it. It is the same for everyone so put it out of your mind and concentrate on the job in hand – winning the race. Do not concern yourself with those issues that are out of your control. Be psychologically ready to handle anything the Race Committee does whether afloat or ashore, and do not let it affect your performance.

Race management is carried out by volunteers, many of them giving up their time to do the job to the best of their ability with the rules/sailing instructions and the majority do it very well. There are occasions when decisions are made which, with hindsight, perhaps should not have been made. However, these decisions must be respected at the time and, if necessary, lessons learned from them. Race Officers need to appreciate the capabilities of the competitors and what the upper wind limit for the class is before boats start falling to pieces and being trashed, which is not

Happy medallists, having put in all the effort to take the silver at the National Championships.

A happy coach (and author) sees his sailors selected to represent their country!

what the sport is about. Safety of the fleet is a major issue for any Race Committee. Before putting to sea, the Race Committee will have covered all issues regarding safety – the latest weather data, rescue boat cover etc. Make sure that you recognise and understand the 'go home' signals should the Race Committee decide to send you ashore quickly as weather conditions deteriorate.

The understanding of race management as a competitor is very important for your overall success in the sport, so make sure that you keep up to date with any changes that are made – especially on a daily basis during an event.

13
Race Training Programmes

Club/class race training seminar

Seminars can be organised with the help of the RYA Regional Race Training Co-ordinator, if his assistance is required. One of the RYA Racing Coaches will be invited to run the seminar, which will cover a variety of subjects as required by the membership. This programme is normally conducted over a weekend – 0930 Saturday until 1600 Sunday. Two-thirds of the seminar will normally be spent afloat doing practical race training exercises, and the remainder of the time is spent on lectures on racing topics with videos and debriefs of the day's practical work.
A Club Race Training Seminar would take the following format:

Saturday		Sunday	
0930–1000	Introduction, Briefing, Discussion	0930–1000	Lecture on Starting techniques/Ability
1030–1200	*Afloat*: Individual racing	1045–1200	Starting practice
1230–1300	Debrief, Discussion	1230–1300	Debrief, Discussion
1300–1330	Lunch	1300–1330	Lunch
1330–1345	Briefing	1330–1345	Briefing: Boat tuning exercise
1400–1600	*Afloat*: Boat handling exercises then Race	1400–1445	*Afloat*: Boat tuning
1700–1800	Video debrief, Discussion	1500–1600	Individual race
		1630–1700	Debrief, Video, Discussion
		1700	Departure

Race training courses

Introductory race training course

DAY 1	Course intro, Safety & Programme	*Lecture*: Introduction to racing How to prepare – Starting procedure *Afloat*: practice course 1	**L**	*Lecture*: Boat handling – tacking & gybing *Afloat*: practice exercises 4, 7, 8	Debrief Discussion Video	*Lecture*: Race management Visual signals
DAY 2	*Lecture*: Starting techniques	*Afloat*: Starting practice exercises 9–11	**U**	*Afloat*: Boat handling practice exercises 4, 7, 8 then race course 2	Debrief Discussion Video	*Lecture*: Basic Racing Rules
DAY 3	*Lecture*: Basic boat tuning	*Afloat*: Boat tuning serial exercise 12	**N**	*Afloat*: Boat handling practice exercises 4, 13, 14 then race course 3	Debrief Discussion Video	Free
DAY 4	*Lecture*: Basic race strategy	*Afloat*: Practical race strategy assessment then race course 4	**C**	*Afloat*: Team racing exercise 3	Debrief Discussion Video	*Lecture*: Tactics
DAY 5	*Lecture*: Protest procedures	*Afloat*: Match racing course 6	**H**	*Afloat*: Racing course 1	Debrief Discussion	Depart

If you make a bad start, don't get depressed. Refocus on the race and concentrate on gaining places around the course.

Intermediate race training course

D A Y 1	Course intro, Safety & Programme	*Lecture*: Self preparation then afloat racing course 1	**L**	*Afloat*: Boat handling exercises 4, 7, 8	Debrief Discussion Video	*Lecture*: Boat preparation	
D A Y 2	*Lecture*: Boat handling techniques	*Afloat*: Boat handling exercises 5 & 10	**U**	*Afloat*: Continue boat handling exercises 5 & 10 then race course 2	Debrief Discussion Video	*Lecture*: Race management	
D A Y 3	*Lecture*: Starting techniques	*Afloat*: Starting practice exercises 9 & 11 then race course 3	**N**	*Afloat*: Continue starting practice then race course 4	Debrief Discussion Video	*Lecture*: Racing Rules	
D A Y 4	*Lecture*: Boat tuning	*Afloat*: Boat tuning exercise 12 then race course 5	**C**	*Afloat*: Team racing 2 v 2 exercise 3	Debrief Discussion Video	*Lecture*: Protest procedures	
D A Y 5	*Lecture*: Compass work	*Afloat*: Use of compass: line bias – wind shift tracking – course bearings use of wind shifts	**H**	*Afloat*: Racing course 1 & 2	Debrief Discussion	Depart	

Advanced race training course

Course intro Safety & Programme	*Lecture*: Championship preparations	*Afloat*: Racing course 1 then boat handling exercises 4, 5, 6	**L**	*Afloat*: Boat handling Exercises 7, 8, 10 then race course 2	Debrief Discussion Video	*Lecture*: Physical fitness & training
0730–0800 P.T. then Breakfast	*Lecture*: Race strategy & meteorology	*Afloat*: Starting techniques exercises 9 & 11	**U**	*Afloat*: Group training then race course 3	Debrief Discussion Video	*Lecture*: Racing Rules
	Lecture: Tactics	*Afloat*: Team racing 2 v 2 exercise 3	**N**	*Afloat*: Match racing then racing – race course 4	Debrief Discussion Video	*Lecture*: Protest procedure & hearing
	Lecture: Boat tuning	*Afloat*: Boat tuning serial then race course 5	**C**	*Afloat*: Group training then race course 1	Debrief Discussion Video	*Lecture*: Wind strategy
	Lecture: Race management	*Afloat*: Group training	**H**	*Afloat*: Race course 2	Debrief Discussion	Depart

Racing courses

1

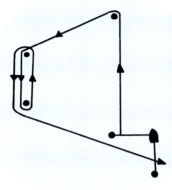

2

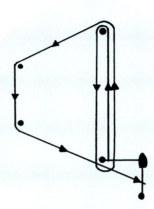

3

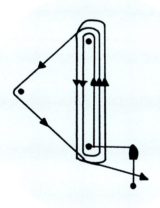

4

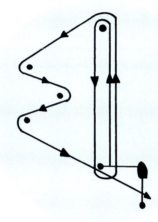

5

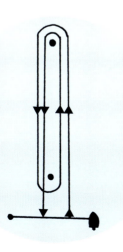

6

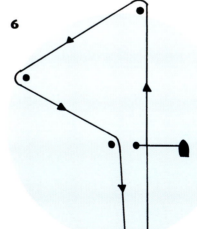

Exercises 1-17

Exercise 1

Use to bring out the following aspects of the sport: boat handling, starting, tactics, rules, mark rounding and sail trim.

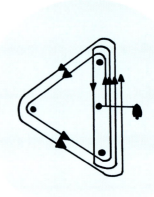

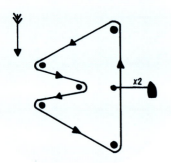

Exercise 2

Use to improve gybing skills and mark-rounding techniques – and also starting, tactics and the Racing Rules.

Exercise 3

This is a good exercise for team racing practice, and improves boat handling skills, rules and tactics.

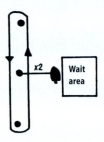

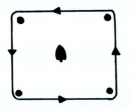

Exercise 4

Boat handling exercise: Five tacks on the beat. In spinnaker boats, hoist at the top-left corner, three to five gybes, and drop at the bottom-left corner. This exercise is used only for practice and not as a race, but the Racing Rules still apply between boats. The coach boat can be anchored in the middle of the square, enabling boats to go alongside to discuss any boat handling problems. Or it can be mobile as required, for video work, etc.

Exercise 5

Use to improve boat handling skills, tactics and rules. Boats must stay within the triangle and leave the coach boat to either port or starboard as required by the coach.

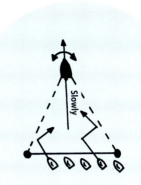

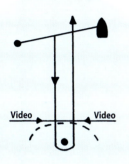

Exercise 6

A running start to overcome problems with rounding the leeward mark in a group, and slowing down to gain the advantage. If possible, have a video camera at the two boat length radius circle to prove *overlaps* or *clear ahead* and *astern*.

Exercise 7

Follow the leader: A good boat handling exercise in beam reaching, tacking and gybing. It is also useful for keeping warm when it is cold or for warming up if you are already cold. Tighten up the tacks at the apex of the windward session, and likewise the gybes near the end of the run.

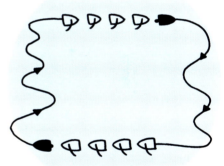

Exercise 8

Good for boat handling skills, this exercise goes as follows:
- Beam reach 'whistle' – close-hauled. Subsequent 'whistles' – tack simultaneously.
- Beam reach 'whistle' – turn on to a dead run (spinnaker boats hoist spinnakers). Subsequent 'whistles' – all gybe simultaneously.
- Beam reach and repeat the exercise if required.

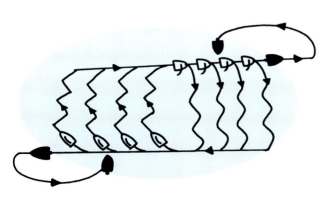

Exercise 9

Boxed start for starting practice in a crowded area, like starts at major events. It is followed by a short windward leg, leaving the mark to port and rounding the leeward mark to port to finish, for leeward mark-rounding practice. In order to work on boat handling skills at the same time, coaches can set a certain amount of tacks and gybes during this exercise. All boats must be in the box before commencing starting procedure; they must now keep their eyes open for the Racing Rules: *no contact*.

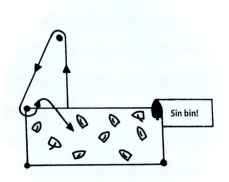

Exercise 10

A good exercise for starting, boat handling skills, tactics, rules and mark rounding. This exercise is normally run under racing conditions, thus putting participants under even more pressure!

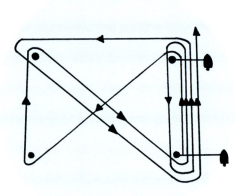

Exercise 11

Mobile start line: After starting, the line moves to windward with the competitors who must stay between the imaginary line both ahead and astern of the coach boats until they get to the lay lines for the mark. The same now applies on the running leg back to the starting area. As the coach boats progress to windward, they also close each other – thus making it tighter for the sailors. This is a good exercise for a group of up to approximately 20 dinghies or 12 yachts.

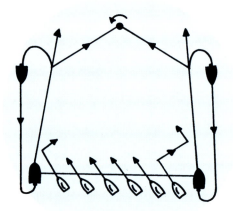

This 470 team is well set up to make the perfect leeward mark rounding, having cleared the spinnaker away in good time. Heeling the boat slightly to leeward helps the lee bow to turn the boat towards the wind with a minimum amount of rudder. As the crew goes out on the wire, the boat is fully powered up accelerating away from the mark.

Exercise 12

Boat tuning: One boat sets up for maximum speed and pointing ability for the conditions, and the other is allowed to adjust controls. Commence the leg until it is obvious that one boat is either going faster and/or pointing higher, then stop. Make an adjustment as required, and go again to see the difference. Stop, adjust again, go again, stop, adjust, go again and stop. Tack and repeat the procedure to the windward limit area, then on opposite tacks return downwind. Discuss achievements, exchange information and ideas to the leeward area, swap positions and roles, and then repeat the exercise. Ideally, on the third test, boats should be swapped to enable the participants to get a feel for each other's boats and to look at their own from the outside. Participants can also watch from the coach boat while a third party sails their craft. A great deal can be gained from such an effective boat tuning session. Working with a colleague of equal calibre is the best way to go faster and higher in all conditions.

Exercise 13

Tacking and gybing: Sail around the coach boat practising roll tacks and gybes while the coach videos hands and feet to establish whether there are any problems.

Exercise 14
Beam reaching: Looking at sail trim, kicker tension, boat balance and trim.

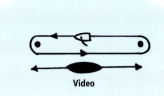

Video

Exercise 15
Having a gate halfway up/down the leg brings the group closer together – good for practising the Racing Rules and tactics.

Exercise 16
This boat handling exercise is good for keeping sailors on their toes – and will warm them up in cold weather.

Exercise 17
To perfect all your mark-rounding manoeuvres, practise the following boat handling exercises across both the wind range and sea state. Focus on your own job during each manoeuvre not someone else's. Visualise what you are going to do before do it – then it might actually happen!

Boat Tuning Log

This Boat Tuning Log should be completed after every race or race training session for your own evaluation and calibration to ensure that your faster rig settings can be recalled easily, as and when they are required.

Boat Tuning Log

Date	Sea state	Sail(s) used
Venue	Wind speed	Foils used

Rig tension =

	Beating	Reaching	Running	Comments
Mast rake				
Spreader length				
Spreader angle				
Mast ram				
Kicking strap				
Cunningham				
Clew outhaul				
Barber hauler				
Taveller				
Jib halyard tension				
Main halyard tension				
Centreboard position				

Appendix 2

Race Analysis

What we did/did not do

1 Technology
- Hull, spars, sails, foils, fittings: are they good enough?

2 Boat preparation
- Did anything break?
- Does everything work?

3 Self preparation
- Am I/we fit enough – physically and mentally?
- Physical fitness – breeds confidence
- Mental fitness – breeds confidence

4 Geographical, tidal, meteorological preparation
- Did I/we check for any permanent wind bends over the racing area due to surrounding land mass?
- Did I/we know the strength and direction of any surface current throughout the race period over the whole of the course?
- Did I/we have the latest weather information and know what the wind was expected to do?

5 Boat handling
- Is our tacking good enough?
- Is our gybing good enough (with/without spinnaker)?
- Is our spinnaker drill quick enough?

- Are we balancing the boat correctly on all points of sailing?
- Are we trimming the boat correctly on all points of sailing?
- Are we in full control of the boat in all conditions and appreciate its handling characteristics?

6 Boat tuning
- Was the rig set up correctly for the conditions of the day?
- Was the rig tension correct?
- Was the mast rake correct?
- Were the spreaders the correct length and angle?
- Was the cunningham hole tension correct on all points of sailing?
- Was the ram set correctly?
- Did we have the correct amount of mast bend for the conditions?
- Is the mast heel in the correct position?
- Is it a tight fit (no twist)?
- Was the kicking strap tension correct for all points of sailing?
- Was the traveller in the correct position for all points of sailing?
- Did I use the mainclew outhaul correctly on all points of sailing?
- Did I use the barber hauler system correctly?
- Was the slot shape correct?

7 Starting
Fixed line
- Did I/we select the correct end to start from?
- Did I/we check on a transit after preparatory signal?
- Was I up near the line at start time going at speed in clear wind?
- Was my final approach to the line tactically correct (no one immediately to leeward of me)?
- Was I on the correct tack off the line (shifty conditions)?
- Did I infringe any Racing Rules

Gate starting
- Did I/we assess speed of the pathfinder?
- Did I/we assess wind and tide to go early, middle or late?
  (also check relevant clauses from *fixed line* starting)
- Did I concentrate on speed and pointing initially after starting to get away from the opposition?

8 Tactics
- Did I/we take the tack closest to windward mark?
- Did I/we take the tack to a nearby shoreline (if applicable) first?
- Did I stay with the main bunch of the fleet?
- Did I use the wind shifts/gusts/bends to advantage?
- Did I get to lay line too early?
- Was I always between the main bunch of the fleet and the next mark?
- On the reaching legs, did I get above, on or below the rhumb line or a backing or veering wind to gain the advantage defending our wind?
- On the running leg, did we get left, right or on rhumb line for above reasons?

- Did I use my wind indicator to ensure I was on the correct tack, not sailing by the lee.
- Was I on the correct tack during final approach to leeward mark?
- Did we go for the correct end of the finishing line?
- Did I use my compass correctly throughout the race?

9 Racing Rules
- Did I use the Racing Rules to my advantage both as my attacking and defensive weapon?
- Do I know the Racing Rules?
- Am I fully conversant with protest procedures?

10 Sailing instructions
- Did I/we read these thoroughly?
- Did we take a copy afloat with us?
- Did I understand them fully?

Pre- and post-race analysis and strategy

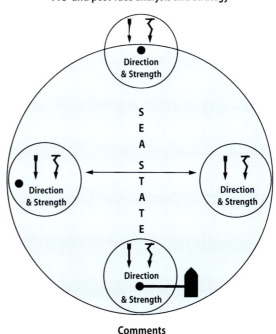

Comments

Appendix 3

Coach/Competitor Communication

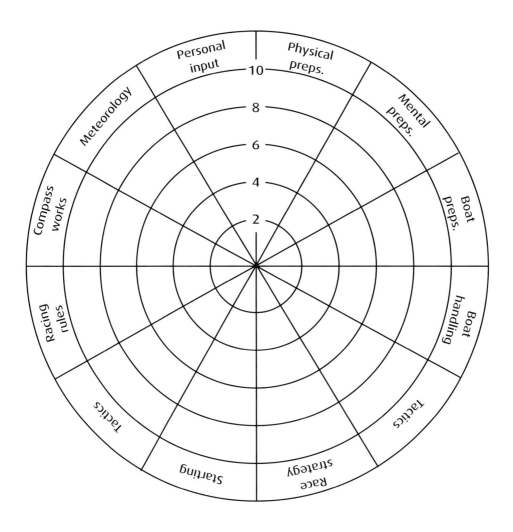

Personal assessment presented to your coach prior to training. Give yourself a score of 0–10 by filling in segments – re-assess with your coach periodically.

Index